the sevenfold yes

THE IGNATIAN IMPULSE SERIES

the sevenfold yes

affirming the

goodness

of our

deepest desires

Willi Lambert

ave maria press **AMP** Notre Dame, Indiana

www.avemariapress.com

International Standard Book Number: 1-59471-034-1
First published as *Das siebenfache Ja* in Germany in 2004 by Echter Verlag.

Cover and text design by Brian C. Conley

Printed and bound in the United States of America.

Library of Congress Cataloging-in-Publication Data
      Lambert, Willi.
      [Siebenfache Ja. English]
      The sevenfold yes : affirming the goodness of our deepest desires / Willi Lambert.
            p. cm. - - (The Ignatian impulse series)
      ISBN 978-1-59471-034-6
      1. Ignatius, of Loyola, Saint, 1491-1556. 2. Spirituality-Catholic Church. I. Title. II. Series.

      BX2350.65.L3513 2005
      248.3- -dc22

                                          2004026529

C O N T E N T S

INTRODUCTION
7

ONE
SAYING YES TO THE DESIRE FOR DEEPER LOVE
17

TWO
SAYING YES TO A LIFE ROOTED IN GOD
45

THREE
SAYING YES TO CONCILIATORY AND RE-CREATIVE LOVE
59

FOUR
SAYING YES TO A LIFELONG COMMUNITY OF LOVE
79

FIVE
ON SAYING YES TO LOVE UNTIL THE VERY END
93

SIX
SAYING YES TO RESURRECTED LOVE
103

SEVEN
SAYING YES TO LOVE EVERY DAY
109

POSTSCRIPTS
ON DEVELOPING A TASTE FOR RETREATS
119

INTRODUCTION

THE VERY BEST

The Sevenfold Yes is for people who, in the midst of their daily experiences, are truthfully and insightfully trying to say yes to life. It is not for those who look at life "through rose-colored glasses," but rather for people who take this admonition of Jesus seriously: "Let your 'Yes' mean 'Yes,' and your 'No' mean 'No.' Anything more is from the evil one" (Mt 5:37, New American Bible translation). To be sure, as human beings, we often experience gray areas. We have to look for clarity and use discernment. But this book proposes that one way to navigate the uncertainty of life may be found in the spirituality of Ignatius of Loyola (1491-1556). This spirituality is particularly accessible in his *Spiritual Exercises* whose fruitfulness has been rediscovered in recent years.

The purpose of this book is threefold. It seeks to:

- provide those who are already familiar with the *Spiritual Exercises* with a deeper understanding of them and offer practical assistance when they make or direct the Exercises,
- introduce the *Spiritual Exercises* to those who may be interested in making a retreat or beginning daily spiritual practices in the spirit of the Exercises,
- help those who are spiritually inclined to grow, even if they are not planning on going on a retreat.

The book follows the process outlined by Ignatius in his *Spiritual Exercises*. It provides both ongoing interpretation of the Exercises and suggestions for prayer practices that will correspond to them. Thus another purpose of the book is to serve as both a guide for the retreatant and a commentary for the director.

This section will offer several introductory comments before proceeding to a presentation of "The Sevenfold Yes."

"The very best." What might that be? If you were to pause here for a moment and ask yourself what you consider to be the very best aspects of your life, then you would find yourself in the midst of what this book intends to consider. And you would also be following the lead of one of the great seekers of all time, Ignatius of Loyola—the nobleman, the fool for Christ, the founder of the Jesuits, and the author of the *Spiritual Exercises*. Ignatius has shaped the piety and spiritual life of the Catholic Church like few others. In recent years, many Ignatian retreats have been offered within an ecumenical context, spreading his influence well beyond Roman Catholicism.

Ignatius once wrote to his former confessor in Paris that the Exercises constituted "the very best of what I am able to think, feel, and understand in this life regarding the ability of all human beings to do things that benefit themselves as well as bear fruit and help and benefit many others." This help comes in the form of spiritual guidance that offers support to people who are searching for fulfillment in life, for their innermost selves, for God, and for a life oriented to others.

To be sure, I am not suggesting that you go out and buy a copy of the *Spiritual Exercises* immediately. Ignatius' little book is primarily intended for the person accompanying the retreatant. If you are not a spiritual director, it will satisfy your spiritual hunger about as much as reading a menu on an empty stomach would satisfy your physical hunger. It originated in a world of words and experiences with which we are only remotely familiar. A classmate of mine once showed it to me when I was sixteen years old. It almost spoiled my appetite for it forever.

Questions for Reflection
What do I long for the most?
What do I "like best"? What do I consider the "best of all things"?
Is there anything I couldn't live without?
What brings me almost to despair?
What are my most fundamental questions?
What helps me find peace?

IGNATIUS AS AUTHOR AND AUTHORITY

The words "author" and "authority" derive from Latin *augere,* meaning "to augment, to allow to grow." An authority is somebody who helps others grow. The authority of Ignatius of Loyola is based on the spiritual direction he offers. This offer is entirely free, made simply as an aid for our personal journey.

The commonly known facts of his life can be recalled quickly: He was born the thirteenth child of a Basque noble family and was educated at court. In 1521, he fell deathly ill as a result of a gunshot wound, and spent years of his life as a pilgrim, traveling from Europe as far as Jerusalem. He then studied philosophy and theology in order to be in a better position to "help peoples' souls." After taking a solemn vow on Montmartre in 1534, a circle of "friends in the Lord" gathered at his initiative in Paris. This led to the official founding of the Jesuit order 1540. He served as superior general of this new and quickly expanding community until he died in 1556. In 1622, he was canonized, together with Francis Xavier and Teresa of Avila.

Descriptions of Ignatius as a child, page, courtier, student, pilgrim, seeker of God, disciple of Christ, founder, and superior general permit us a glimpse at the breadth of his life. But perhaps these designations give even more of a perspective on the tensions that so clearly characterized his life. Ignatius was a rationalist, yet he shed tears on a daily basis and had to muster all his strength to completely trust in the Lord. He was modest, yet he was concerned about promulgating the reputation of the order. He was idealistic, yet he responded practically to other people regardless of the circumstances. He viewed God as "majesty," yet at the same time he spoke of his "familiarity with God." Indeed, the supreme motto of his life was: "To seek and find God in everything." A child who had once witnessed his nightly prayers told of his sigh: "My God, if people only knew you."

This is the source of his authority, this is the scope of what his Exercises offer to assist us. This is what he considers the "very best" gift of his life.

THE SEVENFOLD YES—JESUS AS GOD'S YES

Each of the seven chapters of this book begins with "Saying Yes to . . ." Each one of these affirmations has a reverse side as well, a simultaneous rejection, a saying no. This rejection frequently requires a struggle, an adventure. This structure is supported by the experience and conviction that we become fully human as a result of seven fundamental decisions. This sevenfold structure likewise corresponds to the fundamental decisions of the way of the gospel, the way of the *Spiritual Exercises*, indeed, the way of human life in its entirety.

1. The affirmation of attentiveness, desire and the individual journey: All correspond to the twenty introductory explanations in the *Spiritual Exercises.*
2. The affirmation of a meaningful life, the affirmation of God and of liberation: This corresponds to the "principle and the foundation" of the exercises.
3. The affirmation of reconciliation, of inner peace, of life, of human existence, and of God: This corresponds to the first week of exercises.
4. The affirmation of leading a life rooted in the relationship to Christ, of a life based on the living communion with Christ, in other words, the Christian way: This corresponds to the second week of exercises.
5. The affirmation of love despite struggles and death: This corresponds to the third week of exercises.
6. The affirmation of resurrected love that is "stronger than death": This corresponds to the fourth week of exercises.
7. The affirmation of love in everyday life: This corresponds to the contemplation for the purpose of attaining love and to the various "rules" of the *Spiritual Exercises.*

Do we not discover in this sevenfold yes many of our own desires and experiences? Do we not long to say yes to awakening from the anesthetization of our culture, to a respite from the hustle and bustle of life; to say yes to the space necessary for the dynamism of desire; to say yes to the pursuit of meaning and to touching the divine; to say yes to a process of liberation; to say yes to reconciliation, the removal of fear and guilt; to say yes to a life of growing love for God and our fellow human beings; to say yes to that love that is "stronger than death"; to say yes to the "mysticism of everyday life."

It is fundamentally important to see that this yes constitutes not merely a willful and rational affirmation, but a disposition that is supported by God's infinite yes in the midst of our human existence. These seven fundamental decisions in a person's life are not separate from one another. They belong together like rooms in a house; they are built on top of one another and, time and again, they play out on the ever new plains of life's steps and spirals.

Exercises

- Consider the following questions: What does it all mean to me to be human? What elements have contributed to my becoming a human being?
- Write down seven words around which your life revolves. For instance, they can be names of persons, basic moods, or pivotal experiences. They can be the key points that comprise the story of your life.
- Meditate on this biblical passage where the concept of affirmation is contained in a name or a designation of Jesus: "For the Son of God, Jesus Christ, whom we proclaimed among you . . . was not "Yes and No"; but in him it is always "Yes." For in him every one of God's promises is a "Yes." For this reason it is through him that we say the "Amen," to the glory of God" (2 Cor 1:19f.).
- Jesus does not always say yes, he is not a weak "yes

man." He embodies yes, especially when he says, "Verily I tell you." What are the ways in which Jesus says yes and no in his life, thus bringing the fullness of life?

- Listen to the rhythm of your breath, imagining that you are listening to the divine yes to your life every time you exhale.
- A telling reflection on your life could be to find answers to the following questions: What are my life's seven most important affirmative components? What are its most important negative components? These positive and negative components not only can be people and things which you have had said yes or no to, but also those that have said yes or no to you.

HOW TO USE THIS BOOK

The following suggestions illustrate how the exercises throughout the book can be used along with the explanatory sections as a resource for personal spiritual development.

Write a reflection on the history of your life. Many of the exercises in this book can be combined to create a personal history. For each key event, ask yourself:

- How did such and such an event happen in my life?
- When did it occur for the first time?
- How did I experience it?
- What were its ramifications?

Look for passages from the Bible to support your understanding of God's action in each of these events. Many scripture passages are found in the text itself, while you may recall others directly from memory. By spontaneously opening and leafing through the Bible one may chance upon precious passages. Anyone who owns a scripture concordance can look up words and concepts there and strike gold. In this way you can meditate on scripture as you contemplate your life story.

Practice "simple prayer." If during the course of meditation multiple ideas become simplified and reduced to a single word, you can repeat this word or this form of address during prayer while listening to the rhythm of your breath and thus end up being content with a simple prayer. Certainly, Ignatius would also recommend simply remaining within yourself and with what is inside of you, i.e., in the presence of God.

Practice attentiveness. Attentiveness can become an important method of becoming more engrossed in the presence of God. Consider trying to spend a day or perhaps a week in a state of heightened attentiveness. Paying particular attention to the roles played by gratitude, freedom, a word from the Bible, or anything else that may appear to be particularly important. Additionally, you can carefully reflect for a few minutes, for instance on the way home, on the events of the day, seeking to learn a lesson from them. You can also look for somebody with whom to carry on a conversation about a topic that you find appealing. That, too, can be a form of spiritual exercise that will lead to other thoughts and ideas.

In this way, the book's themes can serve as a primer for those who wish to use it in this fashion, as a set of exercises that will go beyond the individual exercises proposed in each section. What could correspond more intimately to the *Spiritual Exercises* than practicing the art of living?

CHAPTER ONE

SAYING YES TO THE DESIRE FOR DEEPER LOVE

In this chapter we begin with the first yes of the seven yeses that describes our spiritual life: the desire for deeper love. The various sections of the chapter will deal with a basic understanding of spirituality as the desire for deeper love and spiritual practices such as prayer, biblical meditation, and silence. And we will examine the internal attitudes such as desire, attentiveness, and patience necessary to practicing *Spiritual Exercises*.

This corresponds approximately to the twenty introductory explanations and various other methodological references in Ignatius' *Spiritual Exercises*. But have no fear, this chapter is not going to enumerate and interpret the twenty introductory explanations. The goal is rather to communicate an understanding of the spirituality contained in the Exercises. The various practices proposed can help the reader examine the depth of one's desire for fuller life, for growing in love. This desire for life and love is essential, not only for engaging in spiritual practice, but for living with a vigilant wakefulness every day.

According to Ignatius' instructions, three fundamental conditions must be initially met, or at least desired, prior to beginning the *Spiritual Exercises* (cf. Saint Ignatius of Loyola, *Spiritual Exercises* as taken from the *Spiritual Exercises of St. Ignatius,* translation and commentary by George E. Ganss, S. J.; Chicago: Loyola University Press, 1992. Paragraph number 1. All following references will be abbreviated SE with the paragraph number following, which is consistent in any edition of the *Spiritual Exercises*):

1. One must be willing to practice.
2. One must accept that what is at issue is spiritual life, that is to say, a life rooted in faith, hope, and love.
3. One must recognize that every prayer and every exercise aims to structure one's individual life as a response to the touch of God, to God's willingness to love.

Additionally, a number of internal dispositions are decisive at the beginning of the journey:

- the ability to reflect on what one perceives,
- the willingness to lead a simple life and to be attentive,
- an attitude that is magnanimous and generous,
- the desire to attain inner freedom,
- the willingness to patiently follow the path,
- the openness during conversations and a readiness to enter into spiritual disciplines suggested by a director.

Both external *silence*, which is rather unfamiliar to many, and internal calmness are essential to cultivating inner freedom, to listening, and to drawing near to God. For Ignatian life finds its fullest meaning when we let God embrace us and let life-giving love well up within us (SE 15).

GO AHEAD, TAKE A LOOK

Brief profiles of two seekers will give us contrasting views of this desire for deeper love. The first is Benjamin Lebert, a successful young twenty-first-century German author.

"What am I looking for? If only I knew," he said recently in an interview. "The truth is that I have a sense of being driven . . . as if something were following me, telling me: Go ahead, take a look. I just have a feeling that there is something to be found." He continued: "Writing, to me, is an attempt to be rescued. Rescued from what? My goal is to be able to say, sometime in the future, 'Everything is fine,' and for that to be true. But I never have the feeling that everything is fine, that someone has taken me by the hand. On the contrary, one must do that on one's own; you have to take yourself by the hand; and that is so sad."

Or take another young man of the sixteenth century who was not so introspective until he turned twenty-six. Up until then, Ignatius tells us in his autobiography, he enjoyed nothing more than jousting, the pursuit of honor, and courtly life. That changed after he received the gunshot wound that brought him close to death. Instead of performing feats for a secular lord, he now wished to perform great deeds for God and in the service of Jesus. He was, in effect, "taken by the hand" and led to the recognition that "everything is fine." Later, when asked about what fulfilled and satisfied him, he responded in perhaps the most profound way possible: "Give me love of yourself along with your grace, for that is enough for me" (SE 234). "That is all," or as people say in Spanish, *"Ésta me basta."* In a sense we can say that Ignatius discovered what Benjamin Lebert is looking for.

Exercise

What Ignatius called a willingness to practice can be described as living with life's twists and turns as well as its questions:

- Do I detect a faint, almost indescribable, yet continued sense of being driven, of being beckoned?
- From what inner condition do I wish to be rescued?
- How would I want to describe the term "rescue" in one word or in a sentence?
- With what would I be satisfied?

PRACTICE ASSURES HOPE—THE ART OF LIVING

One can play an instrument only if one is enthusiastic about music and keeps practicing. Communicating effectively, succeeding in business, or doing any ordinary activity well takes practice. Our entire culture relies on practice—it takes both "inspiration and perspiration." The familiar saying: "practice makes perfect" can be applied in so many ways. Thus Erich Fromm could write a bestseller entitled *The Art of Loving*. Or take some of these insightful perspectives:

- O. F. Bollnow says, "Practice assures the transition from knowledge to mastery."
- Arnold Gehlen states, "Habits are the muscles of the soul."
- Lefrank's statement, "Those who practice have hope," illustrates a humility that learns by trial and error and gives us hope at the same time.

Exercise is another word for practice. Anyone who is alive exercises. The word exercise presumably derives from the Latin phrase *"ex arx,"* which means to leave the castle of self-centeredness.

Exercise

Anyone who wishes to practice ought to ask:

- What, precisely, do I wish to practice?
- Why do I want to practice?
- What do I want to practice first?
- What do I need to do in order to be able to practice, i.e., what are the means of practice?
- Are there any baby steps? Partial goals? What are they?
- Who should be told about my practicing?
- Is there anybody who can help me? For instance, by permitting me to tell him or her about my practicing for ten minutes every week for a period of three months.
- And after all this, am I prepared to practice over and over (to "adhere" according to the Johannine concept of "remaining")?

In an Ignatian sense, one could insist that the willingness to reach a goal is as important as actively preparing to take whatever steps are necessary to do so. And so we might well ask ourselves, "Do we wish to dream or do we want to turn our dreams into reality?"

EVERYBODY IS SPIRITUAL

Ignatius' second predisposition calls us to accept the proposition that all of life has a spiritual dimension. There is a morality play called *Everyman* by Hugo von Hofmannsthal that is presented every year at the Salzburg Festival in the large square in front of the cathedral. In the play, the character Everyman must respond to Death's probing questions, even while he is feasting, chatting, or flirting. As the voices of the actors echo across the square, every man and woman is personally confronted by the same questions: What is your life about? How is your life going? What drives you? Why are you doing what are you doing? What kind of a person are you?

Every human being possesses a spiritual dimension and these questions address us on that level. The concept of "spirituality" is derived from the Latin word *spiritus;* it suggests breath, wind, spirit. Spirituality seeks to answer the questions: What is the purpose of human life? What is the source of human life? What is the nature of human life? Spirituality points to what makes every human being truly alive.

Spirituality is how we live. It is the manner in which we express the goal of our life; it is our lifestyle. Does it translate into a kind of "bully mentality" in individuals or in a society, which the prophet Zephaniah summarizes as: "I am, and there is no one else" (Zep 2:15)? Is it an extreme form of consumerism of the type characterized by St. Paul as "Their god is the belly" (Phil. 3:19)? Or is its essence in these words of St. Paul "the love of Christ urges us on" (2 Cor 5:14)?

In scripture, spirituality is God's loving breath in us. Its presence is felt when God breathes the breath of life into our nostrils for the first time (cf. Gn 2:7). We see it in the prophets who are "led by the Spirit." And we perceive it in the struggle between the "fruits of the Spirit" and the "works of the flesh" (cf. Gal 5:13–26): between love and hatred, freedom and compulsion, self-centered irresponsibility and life for the benefit of others, destructiveness and constructiveness, deceit and truthfulness. To follow the path of the *Spiritual Exercises* means to become ever more attuned to these

23

impulses, emotions, and spiritual motivators both during times of prayer and in daily life.

For the purpose of a better understanding, one can approach the meaning of spirituality on the four levels on which the drama of life unfolds. Let us use a string of interconnected concepts that work quite well in the German language where an association exists between four words:

- Spirituality is our hold on life, in German we say *Halt,* for the "ultimate mainstay" on which we rely, in which we hope and trust.
- Spirituality is our stance toward life, in German *Haltungen,* our positions and attitudes: generosity, goodness, trust, liberality, forgiveness, hope, as well as the opposites of these.
- Spirituality is our conduct of life, in German *Verhalte,* our words and deeds, our imitational skills, the positive way in which we encounter our fellow human beings.
- Spirituality is our condition in life, in German *Verhältnisse,* the external circumstances, such as possessions, a job, lifestyle, etc.

By pondering this interconnectedness and the distinctions among these concepts we can ask ourselves during a retreat, or even in our daily life, which level describes best how the drama of our life is played out. What is it that we ought to pay more attention to?

Exercise
- What does life mean to me?
- Life to me is like. . .

- What are some of the guiding principles of my life's philosophy?
- What are ten tenets of my personal wisdom?
- What would be the chapter headings for the story of my life up until now?
- What are the most significant events in my life?
- In what sense does my faith and the gospel of Jesus Christ vitalize my life? Or do they seemingly act as impediments?

AN INVITATION TO A LIFE OF EVER-INCREASING LOVE

The third of Ignatius' predispositions is for a deeper spiritual willingness to respond to God's touch.

Every human being is indeed spiritual, but each in his or her own unique way. Despite that uniqueness, there are forms of spirituality practiced by communities and movements. One of those is Ignatian spirituality. It is often said that the essence of Ignatian spirituality is difficult to grasp. This concern is somewhat justified. Ignatian spirituality is complex because our world is complex, it is multifaceted, diverse. Yet, one can describe the essence and the dynamism of Ignatian spiritually quite succinctly: "Leading a life filled with ever increasing love."

Is this too simple? Doesn't this statement apply just as well to all forms of Christian spirituality? Yes, and no. Yes, because they completely describe the center of Christian spirituality in Jesus' own words: "To love God with all one's heart and strength and love one's neighbor as oneself." No, because the formulation "leading a life filled with ever increasing love" is permeated by a peculiarly Ignatian spirit (cf. the section on "Meditation on Attaining Love").

Ignatius frequently describes this peculiar spirit by using the Latin comparative *magis,* which means "more." Those who love always want to give and receive more, not in the sense of constantly placing continuously greater demands upon themselves, but in the spirit of voluntary responsiveness. Teresa of Avila describes rather picturesquely the desire for love that is always growing: "Love is not satisfied by simply marking time." Progress is the gait of love.

Naturally, in the presence of this ever growing love, which Hans Urs von Balthasar says constitutes the very core of Ignatian spirituality, we must ask ourselves: What do I have to do to interact with others more attentively, more helpfully, and more lovingly? That is why Ignatius speaks of *discerning love (discretia caritas)* and offers a number of helpful steps for it. Likewise, when he speaks about life, it is in the sense of a life filled with ever increasing love. For Ignatius the gospel calls us to a faith that loves the world. He expresses this union between faith and life as follows: "To seek and discover God in all things."

Exercise
- What is the center of my life?
- How would I describe love?
- How would I describe my personal love stories?
- How has love been shown to me?
- What belongs uniquely to my spirituality?

PEOPLE ON A JOURNEY

Homo viator is an ancient term to describe the human condition. We are indeed "people on a journey," but what kind of journey? Is our life a rat race? Or are we just strolling along, taking in the sights? Are we like the medieval "traveling journeymen" intent on gathering experience? Or are we treasure hunters? Globetrotters? People on the run? Refugees? Tourists at the edge of the universe? Ignatius thought of himself as on a journey as well, frequently signing letters "The Pilgrim."

Throughout our lives we experience a longing for our journey's goal, for one destination in particular. Our first yes to the invitation to deeper love raises questions about our journey and about our commitment to life's true destination.

Questions to Ponder
- Am I following the right path?
- Which are the ways and byways of my life, my detours and my dead ends? Am I on the way home?
- What would be my motto? Would it be similar to Master Martinus of Biberach's 1498 cry of despair: "I go, and don't know where; I wonder, I am free from care." Or would I describe my existence using different poetic images?
- Ignatius calls himself a pilgrim. Do I have a particularly spiritual name for myself?
- Do I think of myself as a human being who submits to cycles of maturation, growth, and transformation? Do I resonate with Antoine de Saint Exupéry's words: "I am telling you, there is no such thing as divine amnesty that would spare you the

growing pains of life. You wish to exist, yet you will exist only in God. He will gather you up and harvest you after you have slowed down as a result of your actions and after having been tossed around by them; for human beings take a long time before they are truly born."

Anybody who resonates with these words is already on the right path. Part of the journey can occasionally involve making a retreat which Ignatius compares to going on a hike.

"AT THE BEGINNING OF EVERYTHING THERE IS LONGING"

These words of Nelly Sachs bring to mind a group of young people belonging to the Christian Life Community (CLC) during the National Conference of Catholics in Hamburg. Inspired by Ignatian thought and desire for what Ignatius called *magis,* which as we saw means "more," they characterized their longing with a play on words in the German language, *"Mehr Meer,"* mehr for more and *Meer* for ocean. This desire for more, even more than the most bounteous and plentiful area of Earth is the driving force in the lives of people of every age. It is desire in all its forms that keeps the world going—wishes, intentions, demands, aspirations, and even greed and addiction. Without desire life has no stimulation or goal. Think of how frustrating an unmotivated workforce can be, or how cruel the experience of depression is.

Ignatius was well aware of the significance of desire in life and prayer. He recommended that prior to beginning a period of prayer we ought to formulate a specific desire and express it. This is an important and invigorating step to help us get in touch with ourselves and our spiritual journey. St. Augustine once wrote that the desire for God is tantamount to "perpetual prayer." Sometimes desire resides quietly within us, but at other times it is restless until it finds rest in God, our ultimate rest.

Exercises
* On a walk, during meditations, or during prayer one can make oneself more aware of one's desires and thus of one's inner self: "Tell me what you want, and I will tell you who you are."
* If God were to grant me only one single wish for the rest of my life, what would that wish be? To Ignatius it was the request that all his thinking, intentions, and actions be oriented toward the glory, praise, and service of God. He began every one of his exercise and prayer times with this request (cf. SE 46).

PRAY LIKE MIKHAIL GORBATSCHEV

Having looked at the fundamental conditions for a spiritual life, let us look more closely at the essential role of prayer.

The high priest at the temple of Shiloh chided a woman visitor named Hannah, "How long will you make a drunken spectacle of yourself?" Thankfully Hannah shouted back: "No, my Lord, I am a woman deeply troubled; I have drunk neither wine nor strong drink, but I have been pouring out my soul before the Lord" (1 Sam 1:15).

This reference is one of the most touching depictions of prayer in the Bible: To pray does indeed mean to "pour out one's soul before the Lord." This can be in the form of lament, desperate cry, struggle, argument, or even accusation. Likewise it can be praise, jubilation, or acceptance. All of these express the innermost longings of people who seek an encounter with God and with themselves. And all of these are found in that greatest of prayer books, the Book of Psalms.

There are many ways to describe prayer: "Praying is the breathing of the soul" Thomas Aquinas said. According to Therese of Lisieux, "Prayer is like a fire in the heart; it is a simple look up to heaven, an exclamation of gratitude and love in the midst of tribulations and happiness." Perhaps one of the most beautiful and surprising statements about prayer comes from an unexpected source, the former leader of the Soviet Union, Mikhail Gorbatschev. He said during an interview, "[In] prayer one becomes conscious of a certain inner state of the soul during which people rejoice at their love for God and God's love for them."

Despite the many descriptions of prayer through the centuries and the many books on the subject, one of the most significant statements is one of the oldest, from St. Paul's Letter to the Romans: "For we do not know how to pray as we ought, but that very Spirit intercedes with sighs too deep for words" (8:26). Could it be possible that to pray simply means to surrender to the flow of the silent stream of prayer emanating from the Holy Spirit within us, and that only by doing this can we really learn how to pray?

Exercise
- What is the history of my prayer life?
- What are my earliest recollections of prayer?
- How did my prayer life continue to develop?
- What are the images and paraphrases for my distinct style of prayer?
- What types of prayer do I find particularly appealing?
- With what methods of prayer am I familiar? Which are alien to me?
- What obstacles do I encounter during prayer?
- What helps me pray? What helps me during prayer?

LEVELS AND FORMS OF PRAYER

John Paul I, the "smiling pope" who reigned for a mere thirty-three days, the pope who referred to God as "mother," once used a simple story about a family to explain the types of prayer. On the occasion of their father's birthday each child offered a different gift. The youngest recited a poem from memory. The oldest, a boy, gave a short speech in which he talked about everything the father meant to him and the family. Then the daughter, hardly managing to utter a word, presented her father a bouquet of red carnations. Finally, the wife simply looked at him lovingly for a few moments, then embraced and kissed him.

These, John Paul I insists, are the steps of prayer: There is *oral prayer* that takes its cue from gestures and memorized prayers. This is what the youngest child does. The second form of prayer is *meditation,* which involves devoting oneself, mind and senses, to the word, to contemplate it. This is what the son in the story exhibits. A third form of prayer is *affective prayer* that is significantly characterized by inner emotions. The daughter represents this form of prayer. Finally, the fourth form of prayer is the *simple prayer.* It represents a quiet heart-centered dwelling in the presence of him whose name is, "I am who I am" (Ex 3:14). This is exhibited in the wife's loving gesture. Whatever the form of prayer, it must be from the heart and not just lip service. It is truly prayer if it expresses a relationship, an encounter, and a desire for union.

What is true of life is also true of prayer: there are as many different expressions, nuances, and shapes of prayer as there are human beings, levels of maturity, and situations. In a certain sense, we can even say that we ourselves, as human beings, are a form of prayer. Saying "I am a prayer" seems to indicate that "my entire being is oriented toward you." As the psalmist says, "As a deer longs for flowing streams, so my soul longs for you, O God" (Ps 42:1).

"PRAY THEN IN THIS WAY"

To pour out one's heart in "sighs too deep for words" is the primordial source of prayer. Building upon that are other forms and methods of prayer, a few of which are briefly described here. All of them nurture our desire for deeper love.

The Prayer of Presence: In this form of prayer we seek simply to be present to the presence of God, who is both near and far. "He looks at me and I look at him," was the response of a simple farmer when asked about his prayer by the Curé of Ars. In God's presence we allow ourselves to be seen by God. This can be a form of healing prayer in which we allow God to be our personal psychotherapist (cf. Ps 139). We present to God and his loving eye all our needs, fears, thoughts, emotions, wishes, and desires.

One Sentence or Word: Church bells frequently bear inscriptions such as "Freedom," "Peace," or *"Gloria in excelsis Deo."* When the bell sounds, the inscription rings out across the city or the countryside. Likewise a single word or sentence can reverberate in our soul. When distractions occur as feelings, thoughts, or noises, we can respond by repeating the word or phrase. The point is not to reflect specifically on the word during meditation, but to simply allow the soul to sway and ring like a bell. In this fashion, we can abide with the Word, remaining with Christ in the sense described in John's gospel. The method is simply to repeatedly form a single word without much emphasis, as Ignatius did with the Jesus Prayer ("Lord Jesus Christ, son of God, have mercy on me, a sinner"). We can do the same by continually reciting the Lord's Prayer. For the spiritually alive Simone Weil, who purposely used to pause at the entrances to churches, the "Our Father" was an important prayer. She believed that a single "Our Father," recited regularly and with great attentiveness, could change a human being and lead him or her to God. One could recite the "Our Father" repeatedly and devoutly in this way for twenty minutes or even an hour, following Jesus' own instructions: "Pray then in this way" (Mt 6:9).

THE IGNATIAN STEPS OF BIBLICAL MEDITATION

Frequently, meditation occurs spontaneously: whenever an expectant mother experiences oneness with her child, whenever two people are engaged in profound conversation and understand one another, whenever somebody reflects quietly and silently on the essential questions of his or her life. During a retreat, this happens with somewhat greater precision and over a longer period of time. Ignatius' path of meditation looks somewhat like this:

Prefatory Remarks—Remote Preparation: Select a topic, perhaps even the night before. Select a passage from the Bible or a telling event in one's life. Read the passage and reflect on it. Upon rising in the morning, you may wish to recall the passage from memory.

The Location—Getting into the Proper Mood: Consciously select a specific (perhaps always the same) place for meditation and prayer—on a chair or a hassock, in a comfortable and helpful position. It is here that you will experience a broadening of your consciousness as a result of "positioning" yourself within the universe—before God and in God.

For Ignatius, the spiritual orientation is effected by a "general preparatory prayer" that remains always the same; in it he asks God "for the grace that all [his] intentions, actions, and operations may be ordered purely to the service and praise of the Divine Majesty" (SE 46). Prior to the actual beginning, Ignatius encourages the praying person to express his or her desire for this special time of prayer. He firmly believes in the power of wishes coming from the heart.

The Word—Introducing the Text: The terms "text" and "word" refer here not only to the word of the gospel but also to the word of life, the message of life. At first, the texts are brought to life by a slow and careful reading. During this reading and right after it the location is set up by calling to mind the scenery or the setting that frames the reading as directly and concretely as possible.

The Conversation—Active Encounter: The point here is to actively encounter the text or the reality that would like to reveal itself through the reading, that is the reality I am searching for in this passage. What will be helpful is an effort to take note as vividly as possible of the persons in the text and the dramatic nature and direction of the event; to pause longer at important junctures; to stay with whatever appeals to you, excites you, speaks to you, raises questions and fascinates you; or even to deal with that which initially resists you like a tough nut whose tasty meat cannot always be removed immediately from its shell. This is the reasons why Ignatius values repeated reflections.

As soon as the meditation changes to an inner encounter, Ignatius invites us to a *dialog:* with God, with Christ, with Mary, or with persons from days past who had also practiced meditation. This lends additional intensity and direction to the inner movements. The conversation can conclude with a familiar word of prayer, such as the Lord's Prayer, a bow, crossing oneself, etc.

The Epilogue—Retrospection and Evaluation: After ending the time devoted to prayer, Ignatius asks us to look back one more time to the time of prayer for several minutes: How was the time of prayer? Is there anything that is particularly striking? Are there any after-effects? Which prayer sections would I like to put down on paper, using a few key words or phrases in order to insure a greater after-effect? Is there anything that I would like to see continued in my daily life?

Considering the many large and small steps in prayer, one may easily lose one's rhythm, like a centipede too intent on coordinating the movements of its feet with its brain. That is the reason why it is so important to understand and emphasize that the meaning of meditation is merely to enter into as lively as possible an encounter with one's self and the spirit of God.

Conceivably, some people may not be able to work as efficiently with inner images, but would do better with analogies, stories, etc. To those, Ignatius would say: "Take advantage of whatever is most helpful in a given situation." And if you feel the need for simplification and deepening, then you ought to yield to this urge. Repeated reflections should be helpful in these cases.

MEANING-FILLED WAYS OF MEDITATING ON THE SCRIPTURES

It is essential to hold one's ear to the word like a seashell, to use the word like a flashlight and shine it on life, to use it experimentally as if it were part of

instructions on performing a certain task, to understand it as a question per se. There are many ways one
can approach life through the scriptures. Here are a
few examples:

- Continuously cover up words of the text and then
  uncover them one after another. By reading sys-
  tematically and attentively one will be able to make
  new discoveries at every turn.
- To read the text as if it had been written in both the
  first and in the second person. Instead of reading:
  "And Jesus spoke to Bartimaeus. . . ," read: "And
  then you spoke to me. . . ." If we read a text in this
  fashion, it will reveal a great deal more of its meaning.
- The text could be performed as one would do in a
  catechetical class with children. You may act as the
  director of a group of lay actors and in this way
  acquire an insight into every person, into a role for
  oneself, and into the meanings underlying the text.
- It may also be helpful to ask simple questions such
  as: What spontaneous reactions do I have to the
  text? What is the principal message of the text?
  Which parts of the text give rise to further questioning, sensations, memories, and associations?
  Where do I find the most profound connection to
  my life and my own searching?
- The Bible tells us how it wishes to be understood
  and how we ought to deal with it: This has been
  written in order to make your faith in and your
  relationship with Christ grow and "you may have
  life in his name" (cf. Jn 20:31); this has been written
  so that our community and our perfect joy may

grow (cf. 1 Jn 1:3f.); this has been written so that your love of God, your neighbor and yourself may grow (cf. Mk 12:30-32); this has been written so that you will follow the message (cf. Lk 10:25-37; Jas 1:22-25); this has been written that you will sometimes experience healing pain (cf. Heb 4:12); this has especially been written that Christ himself will dwell in your hearts (cf. Eph 3:17).

DRAWING NEARER TO GOD IN SILENCE

"What? You weren't allowed to talk for an entire week? I could never do that." Retreatants find out that silence and becoming quiet are indeed possible. In a civilization where people are inundated with words, silence is a path to acquire psychological health. Thus the Danish religious philosopher, Søren Kierkegaard, impressed upon a young physician: "First, create silence—as a precondition to any kind of healing." In a different context he declared that silence is a definite component of the way of prayer: "The more absorbed I became in prayer and the more inward I turned, the less I had to say. Finally, I fell completely silent. And I became a listener, a state that contrasts with speaking even more. . . . Indeed, praying does not mean to listen to oneself speak, but to fall silent and wait until one hears God's voice."

How do we hear God? At times, we hear God's silence in our silence. Time and again we can sense his message in our own thoughts and in the "discernment of the spirits" that helps us decide if our inner movements and emotions are inspired by the "good spirit." God chose our human language as his own. His

SAYING YES TO THE DESIRE FOR DEEPER LOVE

creation is his word. Every human being is his word. All events are his word. Someone once formulated it sensitively as "God embraces us through reality." Therefore, prayer and silence and listening mean essentially that we need to allow ourselves to embrace the reality in which God wishes to encounter us.

Exercise
* What can help us to become silent? Just as there are many sources for noise, silence, too, can be brought on by various things. In everyday life, this can be a brief, daily walk; careful listening (silence is a precondition to listening); the "discovery of slowness" in the midst of life's hustle and bustle; the conscious enjoyment of a half a minute's pause between two telephone calls; any recurring attentive conversation with spouses, children, and friends.
* During retreats, what helps us become silent is the experience of the silence of other people, long walks, "silent adoration," dwelling in the presence of God who is both "near" and "far," repeated recitation of certain prayers, physical exercises such as eutony or yoga, etc.
* What does Ignatius expect from all this? That we "enjoy a freer use of our natural faculties for seeking diligently what we so ardently desire" (SE 20), namely "to approach and attain to" God (SE 20).

How to Deal with Distractions

"Thousands of distractions again today," I once complained to a retreat director. I wasn't exaggerating. During the silence of prayer, thousands of thoughts, emotions, and questions may surface. How should one deal with these "pests"? There are several solutions:

- Consider distractions normal. A housewife who is meditating on "the fire of the Holy Spirit" may suddenly wonder if she had turned off the gas stove.
- If the same thoughts keep entering your mind, you may try to figure out the reason for that. It could be that a previously ignored question keeps popping up.
- Relax your breathing at the beginning of a period of meditation. It may help to look out the window for a few minutes as you try to become aware of your breathing or your body. Or perhaps use the same introductory pattern each time, for instance, a favorite prayer.
- Simply allow your thoughts to come and go like clouds in the sky. Orient yourself toward the "blue of the sky," determine if the clouds are chasing each another, if everything is hidden by fog, if you can make out a ray of the sun in the distance. However, do not become engrossed by the traveling clouds, don't play imaginary games with the cloud formations.

Francis de Sales once observed: "If your heart wanders or suffers, return it carefully to its original place and move it gently into the presence of the Lord. And if you haven't ever accomplished anything in life other than returning your heart into the presence of our God, and even if it ran off again after each attempt at reeling it in, you still would have fulfilled your life well."

EXTERNAL AND INTERNAL ASPECTS OF PRAYER

In "supplements" to the *Spiritual Exercises,* Ignatius speaks frequently of "external matters" which can be helpful to forming our "internal disposition." Some of these are:

Posture: One ought to assume whatever position for prayer that proves most helpful, whether sitting, standing, lying down, etc. A unique prayer position that I sometimes recommend, if one is so inclined, is to lie down in a corner like a dog, "resting against" the one who invites us to find rest in his presence (cf. Mt 11:28).

Diet: Be modest when you eat. Eat slowly, savoring each individual bite. Or eat less to realize how wonderful it is to have something to eat at all.

Fasting: In itself, fasting during retreats makes sense only if one is experienced, if it does not turn into a constant struggle, or if it helps us mentally without preoccupying us.

Light: Pay attention also to light and darkness whenever they support your mood or complement your meditations. A candle, a picture, or even a completely empty room may also be helpful in this endeavor. Trying any one of these will help you find out which of these is the most helpful.

Books: Ignatius does not recommend reading a lot during a retreat. However, reading a few Scripture passages or brief biographies of saints may be helpful.

Nature: Frequently, nature offers its own peculiarly calming, healing power and a message all its own. Many an excercitant understands what the great man of prayer, Bernard of Clairvaux, meant when he said that the trees in the forest taught him more than his spiritual teachers.

Walking: Pascal may have exaggerated when he stated that there were no problems that couldn't be solved on a walk; still, many people have experienced the relaxing effects of walking or strolling.

Others: Even fellow retreatants might occasionally be an annoyance yet they will almost always encourage you and silently bestow a sense of community. In fact, frequently the sense of community arises precisely on account of the need to be together in silence.

Dreams: Quite a few exercitants experience vivid dreams during retreats. Some are so lucid that they are self-explanatory. Others, however, beg further questions: How did I feel when I was dreaming? In which previous or present-day situations do I feel similarly? Even without relying on specific dream analysis, it is possible to discover a few answers. Experience teaches us that it will always be beneficial to wake up in the morning and take a look at the kinds of feelings, words, images, and hopes that are still on our minds. This rouses our vigilance and may at times provide us with special clarity and internal direction.

Silence: The most significant experience during exercises is the silence that listens. If it is true what Thomas Aquinas says, namely that the "inability to be silent is a daughter of despair," what, then, are the kinds of despair hiding behind my inability to be silent? What is my inner noise covering up?

In conclusion, we could also ask if we are paying enough attention to cultivating "external things" as aids to inner events during our normal everyday life and encounters with others.

TWENTY-FOUR HOURS A DAY

During a retreat everything is important, no matter when and where it occurs, be it during times of prayer, during an accompanying conversation, during breaks, on walks, at meals, in dreams, etc. That is why a schedule that provides a structure for each day and allows time for each element is so important. While an overall atmosphere of silence and of quiet time characterizes the entire time of a retreat, the most significant structural element is the four hours set aside for meditation. Anybody who feels a need may add a fifth hour of prayer in the form of a nightly meditation, just as Ignatius occasionally did.

Ignatius suggests we conclude each time of prayer with a reflection during which we look back, summoning up the most important elements and taking notes. A fixed element of the retreat is also the daily conversation with a director (approximately 20-50 minutes). There everything that has "moved one" is discussed, and the director provides instructions for the road ahead.

Many exercitants consider the daily experience of the Eucharist in the company of their fellow exercitants as an essential element of the retreat. Reconciliation, if offered, also provides many with an experience primary to their retreat.

A day's structure may be likened to a framework, a support structure, not something as restrictive as body armor. That is why it can also be kept flexible without any danger of losing its supportive function as long as the director agrees.

We can learn much from the daily structure of a retreat about prayer in everyday life. As on a retreat, we need an overall structure to give balance to our day. We may well ask ourselves:

- Do I spend my days in a breathless frenzy, only to collapse in the evening?
- Are there meaningful segments in the make-up of my day, week, or a month?
- How much time do I spend on each element?
- What is the best gauge of assigning a specific time value to each thing?

C H A P T E R   T W O

SAYING YES TO A LIFE ROOTED IN GOD

Can I say yes to a life rooted in God? To do so I must first say yes first to myself, then to my life and the world, and then to God in all of these. "The acceptance of one's self," as Romano Guardini once put it, "is the precondition for all human, spiritual vitality." Nothing can be accomplished without it. It is the foundation of life—human and Christian. Each of us must say our own yes, a fact for which we should be grateful. This yes is the subject of Ignatius' "Principles and Foundations" in the *Spiritual Exercises*.

SPEAK, SO THAT I CAN SEE YOU

It may seem surprising that the question of saying yes to life rooted in God is followed by a discussion of conversation. Yet this is exactly the sequence found in the *Spiritual Exercises*. The principle sentence is followed by a significant, frequently cited, preliminary word about conversation. The Latin phrase, *Loquere ut videam te*, ("Speak so that I can see you,") says a lot about the importance of open conversation. By speaking freely, we reveal ourselves and allow ourselves to be seen.

Ignatius' comments address the situation of a retreatant and a director who are engaged in dialogue over an extended period—often thirty days. Sometimes the retreat is abbreviated to eight days, or according to what is called the "nineteenth annotation," on a regular basis over an extended period, but not away from one's ordinary setting. This practice is often called a retreat in everyday life. The retreatant meets with a director perhaps once a week or more. Beyond these formal settings, spiritual conversation can take place with a spiritual director, confessor, companion, or spouse.

Daily conversation while making the Exercises will affect the benefits we derive from them. The opportunity to communicate freely and in full confidence one's darkest secrets and most beautiful truths is a precious experience. At the beginning of his *Spiritual Exercises*, Ignatius points out emphatically that the spiritual adviser and the exercitant give one another a gift when they interact benevolently and engage in the effort to understand one another. "That both the giver and the maker of the *Spiritual Exercises* may be a greater help and benefit to each other, it should be presupposed that every good Christian ought to be more eager to put a good interpretation on a neighbor's statement than to condemn it" (SE 22).

The daily individual conversation during the Exercises should last approximately three quarters of an hour. The subject is anything that moves us in terms of our inner emotions, sensations, perceptions, dreams, images, questions, or thoughts. It might be helpful to prepare some notes prior to the conversation. If some obstacle surfaces during the conversation, the best strategy is to address it as soon as possible. Inner unrest and fears often disappear the moment one addresses them.

The substance of the conversation rests normally with the retreatant. The instructions and exercises that the director provides for additional prayer ought to be rather brief, "for what fills and·satisfies the soul consists, not in knowing much, but in our understanding the realities profoundly and in savoring them interiorly." (SE 22)

Exercises

Since the effectiveness of the Exercises depends on the quality of a helpful conversation, it is worthwhile to reflect on one's daily conversational style:

- Do I listen well?
- Do my questions probe more deeply?
- Do I share something about myself, or is some kind of fear preventing me from doing so?
- Am I able to stand by my feelings and opinions?
- Am I able to say "I" when I speak?
- Am I working on my language and vocabulary skills?
- Am I a compulsive talker?
- Do I dominate many conversations?
- What do I consider a "good conversation"?

Anybody who learns from these questions and practices the answers may experience the truth of Ignatius' words: "Love consists in a mutual communication between the two persons" (SE 231).

PRINCIPLE AND FOUNDATION

In the *Spiritual Exercises* the text of the so-called "Principle and Foundation "(SE 23) comprises only one page; however, it represents something like a blueprint, a foundation for everything that follows. It deals with the simplest and most fundamental questions: What is the meaning of human life? Who is God? How will I obtain the freedom to live and shape my life in accordance with the loving will of God? These three questions will guide our reflections for this chapter.

Our response to them is the basis for our yes to a life rooted in God.

What is the meaning of life? It may be beneficial to consider the first sentence of the "Principle and Foundation" as we struggle with this question: "Human beings are created to praise, reverence, and serve God our Lord, and by means of doing this save their souls." Ignatius elaborates:

> The other things on the face of the earth are created for human beings, to help them in the pursuit of the end for which they are created. From this it follows that we ought to use these things to the extent that they help us toward our end, and free ourselves from them to the extent that they hinder us from it. To attain this it is necessary to make ourselves indifferent to all created things, in regard to everything which is left to our free will and is not forbidden. Consequently, on our own part we ought not to seek health rather than sickness, wealth rather than poverty, honor rather than dishonor, a long life rather than a short one, and so on in all other matters. Rather, we ought to desire and choose only that which is more conducive to the end for which we are created.

As basic as this text may be, the whole idea of indifference may seem strange in some ways. We will explore this further later in the chapter, but to begin, let us consider the following question as a starting point for meditation: How would I sum up my principle and foundation on one page?

THE MEANING OF LIFE: PRAISE, REVERENCE, AND SERVICE

"What makes your life meaningful?" A natural scientist and a computer specialist on retreat were quick to answer: "The moment it dawns on me how the world functions," the scientist responded. "When I do something that benefits other people . . . and God," the computer analyst said. What would your response be to this question about meaning in life? It is not a question we should answer hastily. Our answers may be similar to those just mentioned, or we may have doubts about the meaning of life. How can a life that ends in death and is characterized by suffering and so many acts of madness have meaning?

Nobody can answer in your place. Still, Ignatius' answer in the *Spiritual Exercises* (SE 23) may provide hints and directions: "Human beings are created to praise, reverence, and serve God our Lord." To praise God we must first make room for God in our life. We must allow time for the majestic and the beautiful, and we must cultivate a sensibility for it. In order to reverence we must possess a sense of greatness, an ability to marvel and to be humble, to acknowledge the greatness even in small things, be they full of human complexity or something as simple as a blade of grass. To serve means to live in solidarity with others and to find fulfillment by existing for one another.

Practice the Search for Meaning
* What do I experience as meaningful?
* Could I be more attentive, more kind, more respectful, and more reverent toward other human

beings and the environment, thus gaining a greater understanding of the meaning of life?

* Could I become involved in something meaningful more frequently, even if it means I may be taken advantage of sometimes? Perhaps I would find that in the end, what really makes sense is being there for one another.
* Perhaps a lack of meaning will teach us that there must be something more to life. Or, as St. Augustine said about the longing for more: "My heart is restless until it rests in you."

NEVER FORGET THAT LIFE IS GLORIOUS

These words by the poet Rainer Maria Rilke remind us what is most basic in saying yes to a life and love rooted in God. They instruct us on how to look at life and explore the ways in which it can be approached. They tell us: Life is worth living. The eyes and the heart can become intoxicated with the beauty in the world and in nature. People can become overwhelmed by the joy of experiencing the mystery of giving and receiving love. Throughout our lives, we keep marveling at the existence of life and the non-existence of nothingness. Religious experiences and encounters with the divine—whether they be frequent, rare, or once in a lifetime—bestow on us infinite closeness, expansiveness, illumination, and ineffable personal affirmation. Likewise the realms of art, music, literature, research, technology, and adventure offer more riches than we can take in. In these experiences it is the gift of transparence that we appreciate more than the experience of transcendence. It is the manifestation of the reality of God's divinity in the world rather than beyond it.

We don't always have to have extraordinary experiences. A walk at seven o'clock in the morning when the world is still quiet can offer freshness, peace, and joy of life. Work well done, a satisfying conversation, the joy of a good meal, a well-taught class, time spent with friends, looking at a child—all these can bestow on us glimpses of paradise and dreams of the "heavenly Jerusalem."

Exercise: "Never forget. . ."
It appears that we are threatened by "forgetfulness." We must take measures against forgetting the purpose of our existence, against a life of forgetfulness.
- Are there any splendid moments in my life?
- Is there anything I would never want to forget?
- Do I sense a "fundamental agreement" with life or perhaps . . . a discouragement?

Who Is God?

I remember a theology student who once confided in me: "When I was four years old, I kept asking my parents, acquaintances, and relatives about God. But they acted so strangely that I decided never to ask adults about God again." Perhaps the hesitancy of those adults was due to their own lack of awareness of God and the purpose of our lives. We may well ask ourselves: "How in touch am I with myself, with God, and with my questions about God?" The experience of the *Spiritual Exercises* invites us to engage both the child and the adult in us in a conversation about God. Even more, it is an opportunity to open ourselves to and direct ourselves toward God.

Opening ourselves to God involves accepting our questions and reflecting on them. Some of them may be found here:

- What are all the things and concepts that mean "God" to me?
- What are my earliest memories of God?
- How was I taught about God?
- What kind of images and feelings about God are inside me?
- If I have ever experienced God, when did that happen?
- Are there any experiences, thoughts, words, stories, or people that I associate with God?
- What will it take for me to refer to something as divine?
- What would it mean to me to live without God?
- Would I live differently if there were no God?
- What does it mean to me to be living with God?
- Is there anything I have always wanted to tell God?

Images and Names of God

The Christian tradition has many images and names for God. Which of these appeals to me? God is the highest good, the one beyond whom nobody can imagine anything greater. Nothing exists without God. He is the source of all existence, the absolute being; the almighty, the unfathomable mystery. He is both everything and nothing; he is both near and far; he is the eternal one.

Paradoxically, Ignatius speaks frequently about God's "divine majesty" as well as about intimacy with God, *familiaritas cum Deo*. He writes that he can find

God "at every moment." For Ignatius, God is simultaneously "Creator and Lord" and friend. He reveals himself through Christ as a "generous and kind king" (SE 94), who does not impose on people, but is "begging a favor . . . in the way one friend speaks to another"(SE 54).

Ignatius likewise finds God in the ordinary. Seeing a cluster of three blossoms, looking at the face of a human being, or gazing at the night sky can pull him "forcefully" into the infinite mystery of the triune God.

Other distinctive images of God are inspired more by scripture, for instance: God is love, God is mercy, God is peace. He is the creator of all things, the friend of life, the liberator, the just one and the judge. In the Old Testament we encounter Yahweh, the God with whom Jacob wrestles, who reveals himself in dreams to Joseph, who acts for his people through the events in history. He listens patiently as Job accuses him: "I know that you will bring me to death" (Job 30:23). He allows the prophet Jeremiah to argue with him: "You will be in the right, O Lord, when I lay charges against you" (cf. Jer 12:1-6). Yahweh reveals himself as "Creator and bridegroom," as a friend of life, "You spare all things" (Wis 11:26). He is a lover who lures Israel, his bride, into the wilderness (Hos 2:16).

- What would you write in your journal about God, about your religious experience and encounters?
- Which of these stories and images appeal to me?
- What about the negative images of God: God the fearsome demon, the eternally punishing judge; God who leads wars and "approves" of them; God who is petty in his demands?

WHO ARE MY GODS?

Or perhaps less contentiously, who or what do I idolize? "Their god is the belly" (Phil 3:19), St. Paul once put it rather sarcastically. Perhaps the object of our worship is conspicuous consumption, our own ego, an ideology, a peak experience, another human being, or some other god of our own making. From another perspective, we might also ask: Where and when are we possessed by a "God complex," as H.E. Richter calls the presumption that we have to create the world by ourselves, to shoulder its future, to redeem it. In so doing, we destroy that very world and, with it, ourselves. Wherever fanaticism, drug-induced dependencies, radicalism, or extremism prevail, there will also be tendencies toward absolutism and idolatry.

In contrast to the gods we create, let us look at the God of Jesus Christ. "No one has ever seen God," Jesus said, "it is God the only Son, who is close to the Father's heart, who has made him known" (Jn 1:18). Who is this God, and what is the "good news" that Jesus revealed about him? How did Jesus live with him and in him? His deeds, his words, his healings, his death, and his witness testify to the fact that in Jesus, the God of Jesus Christ cares for human beings as the "Good Shepherd." The heavens rejoice more about a sinner who repents than about ninety-nine just men and women. He is the God of that kingdom whose basic law is: "You shall love the Lord your God with all your heart, and with all your soul, and with all your mind. This is the greatest and the first commandment. And a second is like it: You shall love your neighbor as yourself" (Mt 22:37–39). He is the God present in every human being, and it is there that we either encounter or miss him.

Thomas Aquinas once said: "It is God that we hunger for." Andreas Knapp elaborates on this idea in a poem from his small volume *Further Than the Horizon. Poems Beyond Everything* called "Projections":

I am thirsty.
I daydream
about Fanta, Fürstenberger, and Frascati wine.
Should all beverages, then, be
mere phantoms?
Starved, I imagine
a sumptuous banquet
with caviar, cannelloni, and calamari.
Are these tidbits, then,
mere figments of my overly vivid imagination?
In my longing for tenderness
and closeness to other human beings
I am yearning for my great love.
Will your friendship, then, be
nothing but illusion and self-deception?
Hungry for life,
I stretch to reach
for the inexhaustible.
If there is no God,
why, then, do I miss him so much?

HOW WILL I FIND FREEDOM?

When a goalie in a soccer game is waiting for the penalty shot, he or she keeps bouncing from one side to the other. When a couple dances together they pay attention to each other's subtle pressure and gestures, moving in response. When Ignatius speaks of indifference in the "Principle and Foundation" of the *Spiritual Exercises,* this is the kind of attitude he is referring to. What he means by indifference is that freedom of the spirit which, once attained, one must never let go of. It is the freedom to act differently whenever a new and better option presents itself. Clearly, this indifference does not suggest any negative apathy. It rather prepares us for "engaged serenity" (Teilhard de Chardin) or serene engagement.

We have all experienced various kinds of tension, negative dependencies, addictions, compulsions, reckless pursuit of goals regardless of the consequences, existential fear, and other deeply engrained and destructive behavioral patterns. How great it is that faithful Christians join St. Paul in insisting that we "were called to freedom" (Gal 5:13).

To be set free can be as painful as withdrawal procedures for addictive personalities. But it is worth it to exercise this freedom. Some suggestions:

- The truth sets us free: What are the unpleasant truths in my life? The wonderful truths?
- Trust takes away angst and thus sets us free: Dare to confide more in other people.
- Heed again and again the invitations in the gospel to confide in God.
- Work on developing the ability to do without things. This will set you free. Are there any greater goods that will motivate me to do without certain things?

Ignatius places special emphasis on the fact that there can be no progress without extricating oneself from the endless cycle of self-centeredness and self-love (SE 189). What does growth in freedom bestow upon us? Freedom to love. One of my lasting memories of the "freedom to love" is my father's decision to leave his beloved home and move into an assisted care facility at the age of ninety. "Are you able to do that? Do you want to do that?" I asked. After a long pause, his voice trembling, he said: "For the sake of mother." That is freedom to love.

Saying our particular yes to a life rooted in God is how each of us form our "principle and foundation." This yes rests on our ability to affirm that life has meaning, that God is real, and that freedom is possible for us.

CHAPTER THREE

SAYING YES TO CONCILIATORY AND RE-CREATIVE LOVE

The devil in Goethe's Faust characterizes himself as the "spirit that negates," who wishes to destroy everything that is or strains to come to be. This "spirit that negates" seeks to cause a rift in the created world. Destructive negativity and constructive creativity fight one another. When the rift occurs, relationships collapse.

Across this rift arches a rainbow, the biblical symbol of the reconciliation between heaven and earth. There was nothing that Jesus desired more fervently for humanity than reconciliation. He is God's yes to his lost world, "for he makes his sun rise on the evil and on the good, and sends rain on the righteous and on the unrighteous" (Mt 5:45). And he invites us to meet one another in this way, both accepting and passing on the yes to conciliatory and recreative love. It is only by unconditional love and forgiveness that Jesus says we are made perfect as God is perfect (cf. Mt 5:48). This yes to reconciliation and the renewal of creation is the focus of the first week of the *Spiritual Exercises*.

CAUGHT BETWEEN TRIVIALIZATION AND DESPERATION

Sometimes we may say, "Life is great." But there are other times when we vacillate about life, feeling that "Life is trivial," or even "Life is hell." Miserable relationships, child abuse, hatred, terrorism, starvation—there can be many reasons to make such a negative assessment. These things are not just the result of natural causes, but are due to human activity, both deliberate and unintentional. As we confront the reality of evil, we are often caught between a tendency to trivialize life, as if nothing really mattered at all, and an anguished cry of desperation, as if there were no hope.

Ignatius is aware of this world and its peculiar moments of darkness. He had himself stared suicide in the face; that is how desperate a dead end his soul and spirit had reached. During the first week of the *Spiritual Exercises*, he offers various ways of approaching this dark dimension of life.

Examination of Conscience. One way is found in his directions for how to examine one's conscience. He wants to sensitize us to our innate struggle between tendencies that are hostile to life and those that energize it. It is the struggle between affirming life and negating it, between saying yes and no.

Reflections on Sin. His reflections on sin, on the sins committed by the angels, on Adam and Eve's sin, and on humanity's sin give us a glance into the abyss of the "secret of evil." His single-minded goal in doing this is to let us experience absolute amazement at the love and mercy that embrace and support the life of every human being.

Conversation with Christ. In the conversation with Christ, the "crucified mercy of God," Ignatius leads us to wonder how God, the creator of the world, could be so involved in the world, characterized as it is by sin, even to the point of his painful death on the cross (cf. SE 53).

Reflections on Hell. The purpose of the reflections on hell is not simply to instill fear in people, to "give them hell," but to make them loathe sin and become conscious of what is so terrible about hell: the experience of the absence of love and the remoteness from God. This is an introduction to the truth that liberates us and leads us to the love that redeems.

General Confession. All of these reflections take place within the narrow space between trivialization and desperation. They call for discernment that, in turn, prepares the exercitant for all-encompassing general confession covering his or her entire life—Ignatius took three days to get ready for his confession. Admittedly, this may occasionally turn out to be a difficult undertaking. However, it will often lead to a liberating freedom from feelings of guilt, even a false sense of guilt, and to inner peace. This practice enjoins the exercitant—finally—to abandon all attempts at self-redemption and to surrender completely to the just and merciful love of God.

THE PRAYER OF LOVING ATTENTIVENESS

It is deplorable how much of our lives we waste due to inattention: the sad eyes we do not notice, the glistening sun reflected in a pool of water, the unspoken request of another human being, the gifts and abilities we do not wish to acknowledge within us. Then there is that great blindness Jesus speaks of explicitly, stating: "Why do you see the speck in your neighbor's eye, but do notice the log in your own eye?" (cf. Mt 7: 3-5).

Because of his own past experience, Ignatius was aware of our spiritual blindness. That is probably why the placement of the examination of conscience at the beginning of the first week has become one of the most important of his *Spiritual Exercises*. An integral part of the process of the exercises, it is also a practice that we can engage in on a regular basis. The essence of this exercise is expressed best by referring to it as prayer of loving attentiveness. The following little prayer is an easy way to engage in the exercise:

> *Lord, God, Holy Spirit:*
> *I want to be present before you with my entire life. . . .*
> *I want to be alert to reality. . . .*
> *I want to learn about the things for which I should*
> *be thankful. . . .*
> *I want to find out where I need to turn back, where*
> *I am in need of reconciliation and deliverance. . . .*
> *I want to see what I need to become involved in, and*
> *how I will be able to do so trustingly and lovingly. . . .*
> *Thank you. Amen.*

The ellipsis following each individual request encourages us to pause and reflect more deeply. Some other suggestions for practicing this prayer:

- Experiment with the prayer to find the best time and place for it. Some do it at home at the end of the day, others on the way to and from work.
- Remember that this exercise is simply a normal way to review one's day or week.
- Try to practice loving attentiveness off and on during the course of the day.

The regular practice of this prayer will help us become ever more vigilant, present, sensitive, authentic, reconciliatory, friendly, future oriented, and grateful to God.

DENYING THE POSSIBILITY OF LOVE—SIN

There are numerous ways to describe sin. Perhaps the simplest is as the refusal of love. To sin is to reject life, and to imperil, deny, and destroy relationships. This is illustrated most poignantly by Yahweh's words in the Old Testament: "For they have turned their backs to me, and not their faces" (Jer 2:27). If sin involves turning one's back, then sin also means to sever or destroy the bond of love.

At the very core of sin is the fear we have to be ourselves, the fear that we are a nobody and that our very existence is meaningless. In this sense, sin is tantamount to the attempt to root the meaning of our lives in something which is ultimately meaningless. We say: "As long as I am—no matter what the cost—the most powerful, the wealthiest, the most celebrated, the best, the most beautiful, the most sexually attractive, the most accomplished, the most perfectly religious person, the most just, then my dear soul, you may rest in peace." "You fool," says Jesus, taking one look at these and similar attempts at assuring the meaning of one's existence (cf. Lk 12:20).

The Danish philosopher and theologian, Søren Kierkegaard, once described sin as the desperate attempt, even in the face of God, to make oneself into something one is not, or the refusal to be the one whom God has created us to be. This insight not only describes sin, but also the direction taken by redemption and salvation. What Jesus wants to bring us is above all and ultimately the consciousness that each one of us is "somebody." There is no need to desperately seek to become somebody, to resign oneself to being nobody, or put an end to the "little bit" one amounts to by killing oneself. Jesus' message regarding Christian identity is: You are created in the image of God and in God; you are daughter or a son, a free person, an heir and, as a beloved human being, capable of returning love.

Exercise

* Reflect on the ways in which sin is a result of the fear of not being loved and the desperate desire to be somebody. How do evil and sin surface in your own life, in the life of others, and in the world as a result of this fear?
* Meditate on the dialogue between Jesus and Peter when Jesus asks Peter three times if he loves him. He reminds us of Peter's betrayal while still affirming his belief in Peter's ability to love. Peter confesses his love both modestly and courageously: "Lord, you know everything; you know that I love you" (Jn 21:17). Ask yourself: What does Jesus know about me? And, in spite of it all, what does he believe me capable of doing?

ORIGINAL SIN: "WE HAVE ESCAPED LIKE A BIRD FROM THE SNARE OF THE FOWLERS"

Nowadays, networking is normally perceived positively. But for the psalmist, the image of a bird entangled in a net was not at all positive (Ps 124:7). He might not think highly of networking. And we, too, witnessing the horrifying network created by sin, cruelty, evil, and suffering, may easily be dizzied by it. We know we

65

are all part of a global economy that both benefits greatly from or causes the misery of others. Great is the number of people who struggle helplessly under a brutal dictatorship, in the nets of a repressive society, in a racist atmosphere, in an alcoholic family, in a self-satisfied middle-class environment, or in a narrow-minded religious society.

In German, the etymological derivation of the traditional concept of "original sin" *(Erbsünde)* reveals much about these predicaments. Not only does the term contain a reference to our genes, the heredity that has been passed down to us *(Erbgut)*, but also to original evil *(Erbübel)* or hereditary diseases *(Erbkrankheiten)*.

It is significant that Ignatius places his reflection on personal guilt after his look at "Adam's sin" and "the sin of the angels" in the *Spiritual Exercises*. This likely means that our personal guilt, our "mistakes" and "conquests" occur on the slippery slope of world history. Unintentionally, we bump into others and, falling, take them with us. We frequently create laws and structures that solidify injustice. These may be referred to as "structural sin."

The message of the gospel tells us that original sin has been atoned for although we still suffer from it; however, we no longer live helplessly under this dictate. This may be compared to somebody suffering from a critical illness. It is like the moment when the doctor informs the family that the crisis is over and that the patient will pull through. Surely, the patient may continue to suffer for weeks, even months, and the scars may keep hurting every time the weather changes and he or she may have to take special

SAYING YES TO CONCILIATORY AND RE-CREATIVE LOVE

precautions, yet the most important thing is that the patient lives.

RECONCILIATION—GOD'S JOY

Jesus does not tell us much about God. But he does tell us about what brings joy in heaven, what makes God happy: there will be more joy in heaven over one sinner who repents than over ninety-nine righteous persons (cf. Lk 15:7). When the prodigal son who had squandered away his inheritance returns home, broke and broken-hearted, his father embraces him, has a feast prepared, and tells his older brother who is in disbelief, "Rejoice, because this brother of yours was dead and has come to life; he was lost and has been found" (Lk 15:32). The father simply cannot comprehend why his older son accuses him, reminding the father how he has slaved for him all these years without ever having been offered as much as a kid to celebrate and feast with his friends. Beside himself, the father says: "Son, you are always with me and all that is mine is yours" (Lk 15:31). Many exercitants recognize themselves in the older son who lives the life of a person who "never gets enough" and distrusts even his father.

This is in contrast to Paul's faith experience which is based on his view of Jesus as the one in whom God is pursuing all humanity, even to the point of death on a cross: God "did not withhold his own Son, but gave him up for all of us" (Rom 8:32). The forgiveness announced by Jesus was experienced by the many who recognized the length to which God's love went for humanity: all the way to the deepest abyss.

In one of the most attractive passages in the *Spiritual Exercises,* Ignatius invites us to enter into an intimate conversation with Jesus as the "crucified love." "How could you, God, have gone so far in your love? How do I answer this mystery?" (cf. SE 53). Francis de Sales once spoke of Jesus as the "crucified sun." We can stand before this crucified sun with all our wounds, our despair, our guilt—presumed or real, conscious or repressed. What brings us healing if not the gift of reconciliation?

PREPARING FOR RECONCILIATION AND HEALING

Nothing is more important in the gospel of Jesus than the reality that God's forgiveness and reconciliation are both a gift and a manifestation of God's grace. There is no such thing as forgiveness on demand; one can only ask for it. Similarly, forgiveness is available only if one is also willing to forgive (cf. Mt 18:23-35). The ability to forgive is an additional gift, one for which we must also prepare ourselves.

If there is someone whose relationship with us has been disturbed or destroyed, an internal conversation to foster healing can be helpful. Here is a way to do that.

- Set aside an hour of quiet time, perhaps at home or during a quiet solitary walk.
- Imaginatively allow the other person to come into your presence.
- Pray that the reconciliatory love of the Holy Spirit will permeate each of you.

- Reveal your feelings to the other person, both those that have been expressed in the relationship and those that have not: your anger, your helplessness, your bitterness, your rage, your deep sadness, your pain, your feelings of guilt, etc.
- Continue the process, taking a break when necessary, until everything has been addressed.
- Then listen for whatever response from the other person that might be forthcoming.
- Conclude your internal dialog with the request that peace, reconciliation, truth, and freedom will re-enter the relationship.

If necessary, this conversation may be repeated. It can also be carried on with people who are no longer with us. It can be a conversation dealing with actions for which there is genuine guilt on one or both your parts, or hurtful acts that may have occurred unintentionally.

Such a conversation can also take place face to face if the other person agrees. Alternate between the amount of time one person is speaking and the other is listening. There cannot be any deviation from this rule. Although this method of engaging in a conversation may not always be the complete solution, it will nevertheless often result in steps in the right direction.

FEAR, DEATH, HELL, AND LOVE

"To hell with hell" is not a bad theological motto when it comes to some "fire and brimstone" sermons. Can there actually be a gospel about hell? Can there be good news about hell? How can we talk about hell without simultaneously creating the impression of wishing to preserve it?

First of all, speaking of hell—from a philosophical perspective—is religion's way of expressing the worst possible beyond which there could not be anything worse. Talking about hell provides us with an opportunity to articulate various primordial fears. There is no taboo against speaking of the worst of all possibilities. Whether one considers hell as absolutely meaningless, as absurd, as distance from God, or as eternal damnation is of secondary importance. Likewise of secondary importance are ideas such as Jean Paul Sartre's "hell is other people," or the position that ultimately everything ends in nothingness or in an eternal conflagration, or the notion that finally, it is death that has the final say about our lives. All these expressions are merely different ways of describing primordial forms of fear.

The first step toward reconciliation is allowing oneself to speak openly to God, i.e., in the presence of the ultimate truth about these primordial fears. Therein lies almost the complete solution. But this openness must not only be the result of a fervent search for the truth, it must also be based on the hope that there is nothing that is beyond the embrace of God's love, even the darkest abyss of horror. Divine love bestows upon us the comforts of divine justice and mercy. Is this not the gospel, the good news of the liberation from fear, hell, and death? Perhaps this would be an appropriate theological way to express it: We may believe that hell is necessary because of the existence of human freedom, but hope that it cannot possibly be real because of divine love?

"You Are the One"—Personal Guilt

David, mighty king of the nation of Israel, flares up in anger when he hears the story told by the prophet Nathan about a rich man who had stolen a poor man's only and dearest possession, his lamb. He wants to see justice done. David is crushed when Nathan says to him, "You are the man" (2 Sam 12:7). David had seduced the wife of his commander, Uriah, and had him purposely stationed where he would be killed in battle.

"You are the one." This accusation can be devastating. It may come to us in various ways: "You do exactly what you disapprove of in others." "You are projecting your shadow, your guilt onto other people." "You are not what you appear to be, not what you would like to be." And yet, the unmasking of a self-delusion can turn into the beginning of the discovery of the truth that "will make you free" (Jn 8:32). Dropping one's mask can set in motion genuine self-discovery and true humanity.

Certainly, in some cases, feelings of guilt can be self-destructive or insincere. And guilt feelings may be embedded in the huge network of one's origin, milieu, upbringing, education, reaction to traumatic experiences, etc. Yet, denying culpability, always blaming other people, is tantamount to abolishing the responsibility and freedom that we each possess. The purpose of Jesus' call at the beginning of Mark's gospel to change our thinking, to repent (Mk 1:15), is not to cut us down, but to prepare us for new ways of thinking and feeling, for new life.

Exercise

Without offering a treatise on confession, we can still provide a simple reminder that we live in God's mercy and that the "sacrament of reconciliation" is essentially connected to self-realization, self-recognition, and a life based on this mercy. In addition to an examination of conscience done in the traditional manner, we might ask ourselves these questions:

- What constitutes negative conduct?
- Where am I creating situations that are detrimental, indeed hostile, to other human beings?
- Which activities are hostile to life or forms of self deception?
- Have I sinned in any way against the very foundations of my life?

A woman once told me that she simply loves to go to confession. This said, confession should above all be perceived as a sign that the sacrament of reconciliation is a significant step on the path to complete happiness and fullness of life.

"I WOULD LIKE YOU TO BE HORRIFIED"

Those were the words of a young woman who had spent years as a drug addict participating in the most horrific activities. She certainly did not want me to continue adding to her degradation and consider her an irreparably broken self. Yet she sensed deep down that she would benefit little from some cheap consolation, minimizing her past by saying that what had happened wasn't all that bad. That is why Ignatius asks for tears, pain, irritation at oneself, shame, and repentance during the first week of exercises. There can be no future without repentance and the cry for reconciliation. The proper sense of shame is the ability to recognize when human dignity is being violated.

At Monserrat, Ignatius spent three days examining himself and confessing all the sins, absurdities, and inhuman acts of his life. He recommends this practice for the thirty-day retreat. In it, he has us visit all the places in our lives, remember all the various people, prepare to envision all the dark realities of life, and then entrust them to God. Sometimes, this turns out to be a most difficult segment of the retreat. All this shame, fear of losing face, a mistaken sense of guilt, and the inability to confide in other human beings may understandably turn out to be impediments. Yet, the situation may be likened to giving birth: All the fear and pain are followed by an incredible sense of relief and the realization that despite our failings we are accepted, affirmed, and valued even though we are sinners. It feels as if we have been resurrected and entered a new life.

Exercise

In addition to the review of one's life and general confession, there is the practice of daily confession. In it we admit that we were mistaken, that we have hurt another person; we offer small signs of reconciliation or a simple word of apology. Max Scheler once said, "Repentance is a creative virtue." Thus, an atmosphere of humanity, the climate of new life found in the gospels will ensue. Perhaps the best way to monitor our conscience is by paying attention to the golden rule: "Am I treating others as I would like them to treat me?" (Mt 7:12). How would I like people to treat me? How do I treat them? Jesus says "that is the meaning of the law and the prophets."

To Live in Freedom: The Ten Guidelines

Perhaps, it would be more appropriate to refer to the Ten Commandments as ten messages about the fundamentals of life. They might reveal their true meaning more pointedly if one stated them in a contradictory way to their existing formula, for example that idolizing one's self, lying, killing, etc., will bring happiness in life. We know that cannot be the case. The Ten Commandments are guidelines about life. Quite a few people connect them to concepts of obligation, restriction, and constraint, yet their origin and wording suggests the very opposite idea: the experience of freedom. That is why the corresponding text begins with "I am the Lord your God, who brought you out of the land of Egypt, out of the house of slavery" (Cf. Ex. 20:1ff.). He is, therefore, a God who has only the best interests of his people in mind, showing them the way to freedom and new life. One could therefore view the Ten Commandments also as ten guidelines for the journey to genuine freedom, love and fulfillment. In this sense, one could rephrase the Ten Commandments as follows:

1. "I am the Lord your God. . . . You shall have no other gods before me." You are free if you let God be God and human beings be human beings, if you refrain from making people into gods or turning them or their thoughts into idols.

2. "You shall not take the name of the Lord your God in vain." You are free if you trust in the name of God. Martin Buber wrote that God's name means, "I am where you are." Your freedom is not a product of isolation. Rather, it is the fruit of your trust in the infinite mystery of God and of the respect for the human mystery.

3. "Remember the Sabbath day, to keep it holy." You are free if you refrain from making work and its achievements the purpose of your life. You will be set free if you live in peace, if you grant others realms of freedom, if you do not oppress them for the sake of maximizing profit.

4. "Honor your father and your mother." This commandment invites you to lead a life filled with love, reverence, and respect for other human beings. Such a life is possible only if you honor and cultivate relationships, in particular if you help heal those relationships that have existed from the very beginning of your life, if you practice solidarity and do not dismiss the contract between generations as mere idle talk.

5. "You shall not kill." You will be kind to other human beings if you accept the lives of others as gifts. Do not merely view other people as rivals or competitors who must be eliminated. Teach yourself to welcome differences as a gift and opportunity for enrichment.

6. "You shall not commit adultery." You will be free if you are able to love others for their own sake and if you make every effort to practice the art of loving

with the strength of your own life's possibilities. Respect the relationships of others: the very essence of love is respect and reverence.

7. "You shall not steal." You will be free if you honor the rights of others, if you can leave the space, the vital goods, and the privacy of others untouched.

8. "You shall not bear false witness against your neighbor." "The truth will set you free," Jesus reminds us. You will be free if you remain truthful; lies destroy trust. And lies about your life obstruct your happiness. Lies lead to more lies whose cover-up drains you of vital energy.

9. "You shall not covet your neighbor's wife." You will be free if you do not become a slave to your desires. You will be free if you do not immediately interpret a crisis as the end of a relationship, but rather, welcome it as an opportunity for growth.

10. "You shall not desire your neighbor's house . . . or anything that is your neighbor's." You will be free if you do not allow yourself to be possessed by what you own; if you conduct your life satisfied with what you have, you will remove the sting of greed from your life.

Exercise

While Ignatius has us reflect on the commandments, Martin Luther came up with an ingenious and helpful strategy that continues to provide fresh ideas to this very day. He referred to it as the "fourfold wreath of teaching, giving thanks, confessing and asking favors." Here are the steps:

- Teaching: Strive to understand the meaning of a given commandment.
- Give thanks: Allow a sense of gratitude to grow within for the effects of a given commandment.
- Confess: Examine oneself and admit one's offenses against the commandment.
- Ask for favors: Finally, pray for the strength to be able to live in accordance with a particular commandment in daily life.

C H A P T E R   F O U R

SAYING YES TO A
LIFELONG COMMUNITY
OF LOVE

People say "I do" when they get married. The second week of the *Spiritual Exercises* deals with saying yes to an intimate spiritual relationship with Christ through whom the "goodness and loving kindness of God" (Ti 3:4) are revealed and given to humanity. It is an invitation to say yes to a lifelong community of love. This week of the *Spiritual Exercises* reflects Ignatius himself in a unique way. Most of the images refer to his own experience as a knight: the concentration on Christ as a king who beckons us to follow, who asks favors of us, and who calls us to choose between his banner and that of Satan. Here Ignatius emphasizes that life is not a game, but a struggle, an effort, a conquest of dangers. He is not dealing with a spirituality of wellness nor an ascetical program of spiritual fitness, but with developing a lifelong relationship. In particular, the reflections and meditations on scripture help us to understand Jesus' life and the depths of his heart. They lead us into an intimate relationship with Jesus who is present "in spirit" and who beckons us to follow the way of the gospel. The question that the second week poses to us is this: What relationship characterizes my life most intimately? Or as we sometimes say: "Show me your friends and I'll tell you who you are."

Relationships require decisions, accepting or rejecting a person. That is why this week is fundamentally characterized by Ignatius' observations on making decisions, on the "discernment of the spirits." These decisions form our lives and shape our personal stance on life. Our relationship with Christ also requires decisions of us: Would I like to share my life with Christ? Would I like to offer myself to him, or, to use Ignatius' expression, make him an offer?

Ignatius once elaborated on his experiences as a page at court. It was a page's duty to pay attention to the foods the prince liked best and to present these to him accordingly. This led him to ask: What is Christ's favorite food? What agrees with him? What are his values? Those are the questions that ought to occupy an exercitant; he or she is to figure out Christ's tastes, the one who says that he offers himself as bread for the world. Then we must also ask: How do I like this Christ-bread? Would I like to be bread myself? Would I be willing to offer myself as bread for others? Ignatius believed that the desire to dedicate oneself in this way was the most fundamental completion of life. He expressed it in the form of the following prayer:

> Take, Lord, and receive all my liberty, my memory, my understanding, and all my will—all that I have and possess. You, Lord, have given all that to me. I now give it back to you, O Lord. All of it is yours. Dispose of it according to your will. Give me love of yourself along with your grace, for that is enough for me. (SE 234)

Such a self-offering can only be understood if it is seen as a response to the realization that God has offered himself to us in the same way, through the incarnation of Christ, "in accordance with his divine design" (SE 234).

No Longer Servants, but Friends

We experience Jesus as savior, redeemer, and liberator. He is like the firefighter who saves us from the flames or the doctor who heals us. He offers us a relationship of life and love. He offers us discipleship, indeed friendship (cf. Mk 3:13-19; Jn 15:15). This dynamic is a central theme of the gospels and of the second week of Exercises. During this week the decisive questions or invitations of Jesus are:

- Who am I for you?
- Who are you for me?
- Do you want to come with me?
- Do you want to conduct your life in accordance with your relationship with me, my goals, and my values?
- Do you want to be called and sent out by me, do you want to understand, live, and promulgate the gospel?

Ultimately, it all comes down to the question Jesus asks Peter three times: "Do you love me?" (Jn 21:15-23). In the *Spiritual Exercises*, meditation and prayer on the gospels draw us into the dynamic relationship that John describes in his gospel. "I do not call you servants any longer, because the servant does not know what the master is doing; but I have called you friends, because I have made known to you everything that I have heard from my Father" (Jn 15:15).

The spiritual journey, the way of the Exercises, the imitation of Christ are really a process of making friends. They lead us to converse with Christ "in the way one friend speaks to another" (SE 54). Ignatius leaves to us to determine how we ought to speak with Christ, for one can speak in any manner that truly befits the relationship.

LOVE AND FAITH AND HOPE

Fairy tales are famous for granting three wishes. If you had three wishes, what would they be? In his autobiography, *Story of the Pilgrim* (No. 35), Ignatius writes that he only wanted to learn about the one wish in three parts during his journey: "love and faith and hope." He was referring to the tradition of the "three divine virtues." Human life cannot exist without trust or faith. Nor can there be political activity without "trust-building measures," or economic activity without the availability of "credit"; in Latin *credere* means to "offer trust in advance." Every personal relationship depends on the element of trust.

While the meaning of faith and trust are vital, so are the questions: Whom do we trust? Whom do we believe? Every understanding of life, every superstition, every insane conviction, every leader, every cult is built on faith. Every religiously motivated atrocity is based on faith. "An hour is coming when those who kill you will think that by doing so they are offering worship to God," Jesus said (Jn 16:2). As for Christian faith, Hans Urs von Balthasar expressed the essence of it succinctly: "Only love is believable." And not just any kind of love, but the love demonstrated in the gospel of Jesus Christ, that love which commands us to love God, ourselves, and our fellow human beings.

In addition to faith and love, hope too is part of this biblical triad. It is oriented specifically toward the future. If we hope we allow a place for dreams, visions, utopian ideas, and expectations. Hope means that we do not try to force the arrival of the kingdom of God. The destination is already contained in the journey, albeit still remote. The journey requires patience. Theologian Eberhard Jüngel says that hope is the "long breath of passion." It is strong enough to withstand the tension of living with the "until" of time. It is strong enough to wait for the ultimate victory of Christ's return, as we pray during the celebration of the eucharist: "Christ has died. Christ has risen. Christ will come again."

These three "divine virtues" are presaged by the promise: "I pray . . . that Christ may dwell in your hearts through faith, as you are being rooted and grounded in love. I pray that you may have the power to comprehend, with all the saints, what is the breadth and length and height and depth, and to know the love of Christ that surpasses knowledge, so that you may be filled with all the fullness of God." (Eph 3: 18-19).

Exercise
- How do faith, hope, and love manifest themselves in my life?
- When I read the scriptures, what do they tell me about faith, hope, and love? (cf. especially 1 Cor 13).
- How can I utilize the little glimpses I get of faith, hope, and love in my everyday life?

TRACKING GOD

With whom should I become friends, partners? Which school should I attend? What party should I vote for? How much money should I spend and for what? Our lives consist of so many decisions. For most there are no guidelines, no handbook in which to look them up. The Bible does not tell me either whom I should marry or which job I ought to take. That is why life so often requires the art of decision making. The *Spiritual Exercises* offer assistance for these situations, especially under the heading "Discernment of the Spirits." They are "rules to aid us toward perceiving and then understanding the various motions which are caused in the soul: the good motions and the bad that they may be rejected" (SE 313). Thus we are dealing with the cultivation of three dispositions:

- Cultivating a sensitivity, i.e., the observation of internal emotions and motivations.
- Recognizing and understanding everything that takes place inside of me and the direction in which it takes me.
- Promoting the ability to make decisions, to say yes or no.

This can perhaps be illustrated by a simple example. Three things are important if an animal lover or a hunter wants to observe a wild animal:

1. One must hone one's powers of observation in order to make out the tracks.

2. One must determine the direction in which the tracks lead.

85

3. One must decide whether or not to follow the tracks.

Exercise

Every day, during the examination of conscience, i.e., the prayer of attentiveness, Ignatius insists that we analyze the "tracks" that have been left behind by the events of the day. He invites us to check if they lead toward faith, hope, and love, or if they lead to distrust, hopelessness, or selfish undertakings. And then he poses the question of which internal emotion or direction we would like to entrust ourselves to.

MAKING DECISIONS

Some people insist, somewhat maliciously, that intuition is the ability of human beings to reach a wrong decision within a fraction of a second. Intuition, the inner clarity rising from the depth of one's inner being, is important. However, Ignatius suggests that sound decisions need to be reached on three levels: a calm and deliberate consideration of the mind, a conscious probing and weighing of inner movements, and a faithful, intuitive centering of the heart.

Questions for the consideration of the mind
- Do I look at two, even three alternatives?
- Do I painstakingly collect factual information?
- Do I collect and weigh reasons for and against the alternatives?
- Do I consider likely consequences?
- Do I consider the advice of others?
- Am I prepared to pay the future price for the decision?

- Are there opportunities, means, and people that will be helpful during the implementation of the decision?
- Do I allow enough time for the decision?

Questions for probing and weighing inner movements
- Do I feel internally free, calm, and hopeful?
- Do I feel stressed out?
- Am I concerned about being deceived?
- Does something "taste" like the "fruits of the Spirit" or like the "fruits of the non-Spirit"?

Questions about a faithful centering of the heart
- Does the decision fit into my system of values?
- What is the nature of my motives?
- Am I putting other people at a disadvantage by my decisions?
- Do I endanger my long-term health?
- Do my intentions agree with the gospel?
- What repercussions will my intentions have with regard to my relationship to God and Christ?
- Are my intentions the fruits of faith, hope, and love?

Other considerations
- Would I give my best friend the same kind of advice?
- Could I "die peacefully" with these decisions?
- If I project myself for a while into one or the other resulting situations (or even a third one), which

alternative decision will provide me with a deeper peace, a better sense of myself, a lasting feeling of harmony?

MISSION AND MEANING

One becomes truly human only by being a person for and with others. Those who have no purpose, no sense of direction, no service to render recognize that without a mission in life there is little meaning to be found. "He who must constantly ask why will tolerate almost every how," Nietzsche wrote. Jesus, by contrast, proclaimed service as the basic law of the gospel: "So if I, your Lord and Teacher, have washed your feet, you also ought to wash one another's feet." (Jn 13: 1-20). On another occasion he said: "My food is to do the will of him who sent me and to complete his work" (Jn 4:34). For Jesus, responding to and performing God's loving will was the daily food that nourished him.

What is our mission, and how can we carry it out? While there are many possible answers to these questions, we must be careful to avoid the kinds of mistakes that missionaries of the past have sometimes made. There are two vital components of missionary work that we must strive for: service and bringing a message. As missionaries we should remember the following.

- Because every human being is created by God's loving word, every person embodies the word of God.
- Because communication is the very basis of human life, missionary efforts should be based on sharing, dialog, learning, and mutual enrichment.

- The physical and spiritual needs of others invite us to share the "bread of the word."
- Human beings best seek the truth together.
- A gift always carries responsibilities.
- Every church is or should be a "letter of Christ" (2 Cor 3:3).
- Because all human beings have the mystical desire for universal unity, the purpose of mission can be expressed this way: "so that God may be all in all" (1 Cor 15:28).
- Jesus' original sending of his disciples included both proclamation of the word and service. He commanded them to go out into the world and proclaim the Good News, to heal the sick, and cast out devils in his name (Cf. Mk 16:15-18).

MARY AND PAUL

What a blessing that the Bible contains both Paul and Mary. Paul embodies the missionary who is always on the road preaching, planning, healing, organizing, building, crossing borders, etc. If he were our sole model, most Christians would have to shout: "Mission—that's not for us."

Yet, Mary is also a missionary. She played a central role in the drama of the incarnation. She lived the message of faith, hope, and love in her everyday life. Didn't she believe that the love of God was growing inside her and that she would bring it into the world? Didn't the people around her sense that, too? Missionary activity takes place on many different levels. An important one is through the fundamental attitudes and the radiant quality of one's personality that leads people to report that a certain person always radiated benevo-lence, freedom, friendliness, etc. This too is missionary activity. Wasn't this true of Jesus as well, that he was always out and about, always doing good?

Follow-up questions and opportunities for discovery
- What do I wish to live for?
- What would I be willing to die for?
- What talents do I have, what gifts have I received?
- What talents do others credit me with?
- What needs of others particularly touch me?
- Is there anything which I feel called to, a vocation?
- How can I live in accordance with the gospel in the things that I do?

THE BEATITUDES: "GREATER HAPPINESS"

- "I came down on the side of my friend; it was the only decision that felt right."
- "I sensed that I had to trust my feelings; otherwise I would have been untrue to myself."
- "People gave me a strange look when I asked during a continuing education course if it was possible to attend Mass on Sunday."
- "I frequently feel down, yet people thank me for the comforting letters I write them."
- "It was difficult to stand up for the truth, but it was freeing."
- "We surely could afford a longer and more expensive vacation, but we wouldn't have any money left over for charity."

The common denominator of these statements is that, on one level, they all initially indicate difficulties of some kind, yet on a deeper, more intimate level, they speak of feeling "good." In that way, they are similar to the beatitudes (cf. Mt. 5:1-14). In the beatitudes Jesus blesses those who hunger for justice, who are denounced on account of him (cf. Lk 6:20-26). He proclaims that those who live in accordance with his words will bless their persecutors, they will overcome evil with good, they will treat even disagreeable people with kindness, they will be considerate of people, even of those who hardly notice it. They will not act for the sake of recognition or gratitude: "If you love those who love you, what credit is that to you? For even sinners love those who love them"(Lk 6:32f.). Jesus directs those who are seeking true happiness to search for this treasure in their own personal "field of happiness." Anyone who digs there and finds what he or she is looking for will be, as the French language expresses it, *bienheureux*—blissfully happy. St. Paul assures us of the existence of this state of happiness: "We are afflicted in every way, but not crushed; perplexed, but not driven to despair; persecuted, but not forsaken"(2 Cor 4:8-9; cf. 2 Cor 6:8-10). It is the kind of happiness we can find only by saying yes to an intimate spiritual relationship with Christ, by saying yes to a lifelong community of love.

CHAPTER FIVE

ON SAYING YES TO LOVE UNTIL THE VERY END

There are times when it seems easy to say yes to life and loving. Life can be glorious and love can bless us with a sense of happiness and fulfillment. Still our experience tells us that life is not always this way. Joy and agony, fulfillment and emptiness, light and darkness often exist side-by-side. In scripture we find both Mount Tabor and Mount Golgotha, we hear the cries of "Hosanna" and "Crucify him!" The third week of Exercises leads us into the night of Jesus' loving surrender, always with a view to his death. It invites us to join him on the way of loving, to let it happen to us as well, to the very end "through him and with him and in him."

FAITHFULNESS: THE TRUE TEST OF LOVE

During this week of the Exercises, one should "try to foster an attitude of sorrow, suffering, and heartbreak, by calling often to memory the labors, fatigue, and sufferings which Christ our Lord suffered, from his birth up to whatever mystery of his Passion [one is] contemplating at the time" (SE 206). Nowadays, empathy and compassion are words that come closest to the biblical meaning of suffering with another, pity, or sympathy.

In order to better comprehend the meaning of the meditations for this week, we might imagine the experience of people who find themselves trying to love faithfully and unswervingly. They may be "fighting a headwind," "caught in a dark valley," or in the "for worse" rather than "for better" time of their marriage.

They may be a physician who risks becoming infected, a parent who is trying hard to love a wayward child or a child trying to love a wayward parent, a friend trying to maintain a friendship through a severe crisis, or a fireman risking his life to save a child. Whenever we see such things, it is because of this same faithful love.

Only in love like this can we find an answer to the most persistent and difficult questions of life: Why did this happen? Why did it happen to me? Why do we live and why do we die? Why is there evil in this world? God's compassion shown in Jesus demonstrates that love is stronger than death, stronger than sin, resistance, ignorance, hatred, stronger than every negative force in the world.

"For God so loved the world that he gave his only Son, so that everyone who believes in him may not perish but may have eternal life" (Jn 3:16; cf. Jn 13:1). People lost their faith in Auschwitz. But in Auschwitz, people also found their faith. Standing in front of his bombed-out house, the only survivor of an air raid in the German city of Augsburg told a priest: "Father, you don't need to comfort me. I lost everything last night—and found God."

ILLNESS, DEATH, AND LONELINESS

Ignatius once observed that the careless manner in which he had dealt with his health taught him "how to learn from mistakes." Illness cannot normally be avoided. It has been said that the average human being suffers from more than 250 illnesses over a lifetime. When we meet someone who has been suffering severely for a long time, we may wonder whether suffering through such conditions will lead the patient close to what mystics call the "dark night of the soul."

In the midst of such darkness, one is confronted by many temptations. "Do you still mean to persist in your integrity? Curse God, and die" (Jb 2:9), Job's wife advises her husband. But what if, instead of becoming embittered during a horrible chronic illness, a person remains receptive to others? Job was such a person, and in the end he was able to say: "I know that my Redeemer lives, and that at the last he will stand upon the earth; and after my skin has been thus destroyed, then in my flesh I will see God, whom I shall see on my side, and my eyes shall behold, and not another. My heart faints within me." (Jb 19:25-27)

Could it be that illness is one of the great teachers in life? If so, what is its hidden message? Certainly, it will teach us about how to live in a healthier manner. Perhaps it will also teach us how to look inward and recognize: "All those things that annoy are what is making me sick," or "The more I can share my suffering with others, the less sick I feel." On a deeper level we may want to ask how we are being changed by illness. Do we see some purpose in it? Could it be that the external things that we cannot change cause an internal change in us? Are we perhaps changed more by the helplessness we have experienced than by our conscious efforts? Perhaps as socially-minded people we may also ask ourselves if we could not contribute more to the preservation of health in society on a grassroots level through efforts to promote a more careful and healthy lifestyle.

When Ignatius was on his deathbed he asked for the Pope's blessing. His wish was not granted. His condition was not considered to be serious enough. The final words his nurse kept hearing from behind the door of his room were: *"Ay Dios. Ay Dios."* (Oh God, oh God). Ignatius died alone. Sometimes we are granted strength in our loneliness. Such was the experience of one fellow Jesuit. Among the words that gave him solace at the end of his life were these by the German writer Gotthard de Beauclair:

> *After the noon hour, light becomes precious.*
> *The stars are born in these shadows.*
> *The great silence.*
> *You are just alone, not lonesome.*

"MY GOD, MY GOD, WHY HAVE YOU FORSAKEN ME?"

When, as loving people, we accompany another on his or her journey toward death or when we walk with someone during a crisis, we may sense some of the suffering the disciples of Jesus had to undergo. And, like them, we may discover that the miracle of faith may break through as if the day were dawning in the middle of the night. The *Spiritual Exercises* invite us to accompany Jesus on his journey, to experience how love achieves perfection in the end. Reflect on each of the following words and experiences that characterized Jesus' final journey:

Prepared: Jesus was prepared step-by-step as the confrontations heated up and his disciples left him.

Persecuted: Jesus must have known that some people followed him only in order to arrest him.

Hidden: Jesus, the "revealer," had to hide out at times during the last months of his life.

Betrayed: Is there anything worse in life than to be betrayed by people close to you, by friends?

Sweating: Fighting for his life, he was sweating blood, perhaps questioning if everything comes to an end in death?

Unsure: Has everything that I have done been in vain?

Accused: Jesus who forgave and reconciled others, stood accused.

Denounced: Jesus, "the truth," is denounced by false witnesses.

Mocked: His dignity is mocked to the very core by the soldiers.

Cursed: Jesus, who had always blessed others, is cursed by the religious authorities: "Cursed be he who hangs on the cross."

Abandoned: "My God, my God, why have you forsaken me?"(Mk 15:34).

Reconciled: Dying, he cried out: "Father, forgive them; for they do not know what they are doing" (Lk 23:34).

Destroyed: A cry, a thrust with a lance, the end.

Buried: They would have preferred to bury him for good.

The story of the passion of our Lord invites us to follow his path of suffering, to walk with Christ as we read, to meditate and accompany him through the stations of his life and of our own life and time.

PRAYING AT THE WALLS OF REJECTION

There are rejections we can tolerate with hardly a whimper. However, there are rejections and denials that can take our breath away, that make us feel like dying:

- We want to have something no matter what. . . . No.
- We wish that this and that change could be possible in a community. . . . No.
- Like St. Paul, we would like to be rid of "a thorn in the flesh". . . . No.
- Not just once, but time and again. . . . No.

The experience of powerlessness can make us angry or wear us down. Or it may make us resign ourselves: There is nothing I can do; everything is in vain. No one takes me seriously; I am a nobody. Our inner self feels despised, indeed its very existence is threatened. Of course, the first reasonable response is to figure out how one might be able to carry on patiently, perhaps by renegotiating, coming up with an imaginative solution, or tenaciously working on one's self or relationships. But when this does not work, when we run head-on into a wall like a battering ram, then the strategy of the gospel, the way of Jesus, might recommend itself. He too confronted many nos. As he stood in front of the walls of Jerusalem, knowing that his betrayal and death were at hand, he cried out: "O Jerusalem, Jerusalem, killing the prophets and stoning those who are sent to you! How often would I have gathered your children together as a hen gathers her brood under her wings, and you would not!" And Jesus wept, reports St. Luke (Lk 19:41).

Having fought, raged, and negotiated sufficiently, one might want to stand next to a wall, or lean against it during this meditative exercise. Reflect on each negative response or rejection and simply accept them. Refrain, however, from wallowing in them or from trying to push the wall aside. Instead, simply permit the negative experiences to unfold. Again and again, even to the point where you might feel like dying from them. Indeed, we do die from them in a certain sense. Unlike anywhere else, it is here that we learn a little bit about resurrection. Getting our way is not tantamount to ultimate happiness. We are told about Jesus that he died "outside the walls." Dying precedes being raised up.

A different way of dealing with powerlessness, rage, fear, and deep resignation can be to penetrate all the way to the source of the pain that is hidden beneath rage or resignation. Through this process, we may reach the point where we can proclaim with the psalmist: "It is my grief that the right hand of the Most High has changed" (Ps 77:10). Ask: What is the nature of my pain? What are its sources? Which of my values were injured?

ON SAYING YES TO LOVE UNTIL THE VERY END

As soon as we succeed, we will be closer to the wound and thus the beginning of healing. There is a kind of pain that heals pain. The effective treatment of powerlessness and pain can be understood as what Jesus meant when he said we must pick up our cross each day. A confrere of mine told me one ought to say: "Take your daily love upon you," instead of "Take your daily cross upon you." He wanted to counteract the impression that following the cross of Jesus always amounted to something that would cause one to moan. A better way of putting it would presumably be: "Shoulder your daily tensions, needs, and little deaths . . . for my burden is light" (cf. Mt 11:30). Those who have experienced the presence of the Spirit of Jesus will easily accept this promise.

C H A P T E R   S I X

SAYING YES TO RESURRECTED LOVE

Walking through "the valley of the shadow of death" (cf. Ps 23), is not the end of our spiritual journey. The purpose of the Exercises is not to lead us into the hopeless darkness, but into the hopeful light of the resurrection. This is what we profess when we proclaim the eucharistic acclamation: "Dying you destroyed our death, rising you restored our life." After the resurrection, Jesus' wounds were transfigured, no longer signs of torture and death, but sources of life. A poem by the German poet Nelly Sachs presents us with a glimpse of the healing power of these "transfigured wounds."

> *Cry from your heart*
> *unleashed burden of fear*
> *two butterflies*
> *hold up the weight*
> *of the world for you*
> *and I*
> *enclose your tear in this word:*
> *your fear has turned to light.*

The fourth week of *Spiritual Exercises* deals with the acceptance of the radiance of the light of the resurrection shining into our lives. That which the Old Testament celebrates as the "victory of Yahweh" is expressed in the New Testament as the mystery of the resurrection. This mystery is told through the narratives about the resurrection, in the garden stories surrounding the tomb, and in the sea stories in the gospel. Ignatius encourages us to meditate and contemplate on these stories with all their nuances. Ignatius perhaps expresses the belief in the resurrection in the most tender way when he has the exercitant contemplate how Jesus appears and reveals himself to his mother, Mary. Although there is no gospel record of this apparition, there is an ancient Christian tradition that Jesus must have appeared to her. Ignatius imagines him consoling her "the way friends console one another" (SE 224). Should "true friendship" perhaps be similar to the dawn of the resurrection?

The experience of the risen Lord is described not only in the stories about the resurrection, but also when Paul speaks of our dying and rising with Christ. Paul describes the certainty of faith that he experiences when he proclaims: "For I am convinced that neither death, nor life, nor angels, nor rulers, nor things present, nor things to come, nor powers, nor height, nor depth, nor anything else in all creation, will be able to separate us from the love of God in Christ Jesus our Lord" (Rom 8:38f.).

John expresses the events surrounding the resurrection through the experience of loving and being loved: "We know that we have passed from death to life because we love one another. Whoever does not love abides by death" (1 Jn 3:14). Thus one can describe resurrection also in the following terms: Resurrection happens whenever one loves and is loved in return. Love is God's life in us. This is the love that we are told is stronger than death.

To be sure, the otherwise gentle John continues with frightening forcefulness: "All who hate a brother or sister are murderers, and you know that murderers do not have eternal life abiding in them. We know love by this, that he laid down his life for us—and we ought to lay down our lives for one another. How does God's love abide in anyone who has the world's goods and sees a brother or sister in need and yet refuses to help? Little children, let us love, not in word or speech, but in truth and action." (1 Jn 3:15-18). Words such as these may frighten us. How much death is still left in us? And yet we are also comforted: "We abide in him and he in us, because he has given us of his Spirit." (1 Jn 4:13). And: "In this is love, not that we loved God but that he loved us and sent his Son." (1 Jn 4:10).

MEDITATION ON ATTAINING LOVE

This meditation is one, if not the, high point of the *Spiritual Exercises*. At the same time, it serves as a transition back to everyday life. What are its most significant points?

- Love ought to manifest itself more by deeds than by words, that is to say, what matters is the manner in which we live our lives (SE 230).
- Love shows itself in the sharing of everything we possess, everything we know, and everything we know how to do. "Love consists in the communication between . . . two persons" (SE 231).
- In love, this sharing, this offering of our gifts, expresses the desire to make a gift of ourselves, of our very person. Ignatius attributes this desire to God as well, who gives himself to all human beings to the fullest extent possible, so that human beings, responding freely, will be able to give themselves to God (SE 234).
- Love is "mystical": We ought to imagine how God lives inwardly in and through all creation, whether animals, vegetables, minerals, or in human beings.

In other words, God lives inwardly in the entire world and all the dimensions of each person's individual existence (SE 235).

- Ignatius challenges us to imagine the realm of the workaday world as a place where love can be expressed. It may sound strange to us that God conducts himself like one who performs "heavy labor" and that people act "cooperatively" and "co-creatively" with him, but this is what Ignatius says (SE 236).

- Finally, Ignatius utilizes the image of a flower to remind us that human beings ought to turn toward the divine sun like plants turn toward the physical sun. We are to open ourselves to God's love, and allow ourselves to be permeated by it in order to be able to love more and more deeply (SE 237).

What do these breath-taking invitations to contemplate, pray, and live trigger in me? It was Ignatius' prayerful wish that he "may become able to love and serve the Divine Majesty in all things" (SE 233).

ALL'S WELL THAT ENDS WELL

Beginnings and endings are particularly significant points in life. Conclusions are drawn and new courses are steered. The same is true of the Exercises.

Of course, it is necessary to take a look back to the journey and ask questions such as:

- How did I fare overall?
- What were the highlights?
- Were there any mountains to climb, any valleys to traverse?

- Were there any detours along the way?
- Were there any oases, new vistas, new insights?
- Were there any difficulties or complications?
- What was helpful to me?
- How did I get along with my fellow travelers?
- Did any new goals come into view?

And of course, a look ahead will be equally important:
- What will it be like to arrive at the journey's end?
- Whom will I meet there?
- What will the days and months ahead have in store for me?
- What are one or two concerns that I will take away with me?
- How will I remember them?
- Will there be anything or anybody that will help me continue along the way?

It may be helpful to compose a letter to oneself that will incorporate the most important impulses during the days of the retreat.

"Even the faintest ink is stronger than the best memory." If this saying is true, we may hope that "the Advocate, the Holy Spirit . . . will . . . remind you of all that I have said to you" (cf. Jn 14: 26). And let us say in response: "Lord, everything is in your hands, be it the beginning or the end." For he is the Alpha and Omega, the beginning and the end.

We continue to celebrate both the beginnings and endings, not only through the end of the Exercises but also in our daily lives. We continue to live through "the sadness of farewell and the joys of hello" (Martin Buber).

CHAPTER SEVEN

SAYING YES TO LOVE EVERY DAY

It is fairly easy to say yes to an inspiration or to swear our loyalty when we are on a psychological high. However, our genuineness is not seen until we say yes to everyday life, a life that strives to renew itself, a life in which daily routine does not prevail over important spiritual experiences. "How did your retreat go?" "Quite well, but it took me fully three weeks to get back to the way things were before the retreat." This ironic snippet of a dialog begs the question about what will happen after a retreat. Are retreats and prayer merely an interruption of everyday life? Just another useless attempt at a new beginning? Or are they the leaven in the dough of everyday life? Because the "object" of a retreat is one's own life, there are additional references in the *Spiritual Exercises* to a "follow-up" in everyday life. By setting up a so-called "rule of life," areas are brought into view: how to deal with money, people, food, life in the church, rules about making decisions, etc. Furthermore, all mediations on vices and virtues directly affect not only vital skills, but also the ways in which life is to be organized.

The daily examination of one's conscience and the so-called "particular examination" or "specific examination of one's conscience" are provided to help us make sense of our daily life in terms of the gospel. They invite us to look at the truth of our daily experience in the light of Christ.

ASCENSION AND GROUNDEDNESS

Twice Ignatius returned to the Mount of Olives in order to impress upon his mind the precise direction of the footprints of Jesus. Pious eyes tried to imagine

Jesus leaving footprints on the stony surface at the moment of his ascension. This may strike us as Mediterranean piety. Yet it brings a good question to mind: What direction do our ideals take? Our dreams? Our most profound experiences? To what extent do my spiritual experiences serve as a compass for my every-day daily life? What kind of impressions do my they leave behind on my soul? In which direction do they point on my daily journey?

"Men of Galilee, why do you stand looking up toward heaven?" (Acts 1:11), two men dressed in white ask the disciples whose eyes are glued to the sky. The Easter stories direct them to look for Jesus in Galilee, their new home. Right there. While fishing. In the synagogue. In the family. In the dust of everyday life. Nelly Sachs once referred to human beings as "enraptured dust," capable of jumping unto the "rope of longing" while attempting to figure out the amount of the dust's volume.

Karl Rahner invites us to live the "mysticism of everyday life." The meaning of the mysticism of everyday life is to ask about what will benefit other people. How can I practice loving patience and live a life of "happy tenacity" (Corona Bamberg)? How can I practice both freedom and consideration? How can I experience both "struggle and contemplation" simultaneously?

Attentiveness and prayer will teach us to undertake the daily experiments and learning steps in the "school of God" (Ignatius). The most important step is always the next one. Will it point in the direction that Jesus' feet were pointing or will it point somewhere else?

ROADSIDE ASSISTANCE

Like drivers whose cars break down on the highway, occasionally we need to call for roadside assistance. Recognizing that we need help is an important first step. But each of us also needs to ask: What kind of help do I need? Am I willing to let others help me? The following are a few suggestions for roadside assistance. Pick and choose those that seem to resonate most deeply with your unique needs and gifts.

- If you are feeling alone consider looking for a spiritual community of some kind: a faith-sharing group, a prayer group, a Bible study group, or something similar in a parish. Some people benefit greatly from this kind of regular spiritual support.

- If you need time for reflection or the distance to gain a healthy perspective, think about making an occasional or regularly scheduled weekend retreat.

- Additional development may be achieved through some continuing education courses or workshops.

- If you feel lost, look for a mentor. If you are engaged in ministry or similar kind of work, ask for some supervision and constructive feedback from someone you trust.

- If life becomes overly serious and too somber, seek out light-hearted friends and enjoy letting go of chronic worries.

- If you feel the need to constantly confess to others, to continually speak with friends about your troubles, perhaps the services of a professional counselor can be a systematic way to fill those needs without constantly troubling the people around you.

Real freedom can be achieved only as a result of educating oneself. Thus one makes the transition from being determined by others to self-determination and to the acceptance of responsibility for oneself. What is the use of the seeds of the most beautiful and prolific plants if they are not planted in the soil of everyday life? Without cultivating and tending, the spiritual seeds planted in us will remain sterile.

After ten years of making and directing the *Spiritual Exercises*, I tried to define for myself in concrete, down-to-earth terms, what the essential practices to promote a spiritual life are. I came up with the following:

- If something is working, stay with it.
- Make a conscious and free decision about what you are going to do.
- Seek out the assistance of a spiritual companion or director.

To this day I have not had to rephrase this advice.

One kind of daily practice you might consider is the "particular examination." Ignatius chose this as his simple, spiritual self-help program. It works in accordance with the ancient Roman saying, *"divide et impera,"* that is "divide and conquer." In other words, we cannot hope to change overnight. If we want to become a new person, to change this or that, we have to take one step at a time. For instance, if I have decided to lose weight, I might begin by trying to eat more slowly or to eat less. Or perhaps the stress of everyday life is wearing me down and I'm becoming hard to live with. If I want to change, I will profit from taking one step at a time. I might allow myself more free time, set aside some time for prayer, or spend more time talking with my children or my spouse rather than in front of the television set.

The following questions can be most helpful:

- What is my goal? What do I really want?
- What are my motives? What do I hope to gain from my goal?
- Who and what can help me accomplish it?
- What steps do I need to take to reach that goal?
- Is my goal "small enough," is it attainable?

Ignatius offers three pointers:

1. Briefly remind yourself of your goal three times a day: upon rising, at noon, and in the evening.

2. Combine the reminder with a prayerful request that the Spirit of God may assist you.

3. Monitor your progress. You might set up a chart, leaving two lines for every day, then record on one line at noon and on the other in the evening how often you succeeded or failed to follow your plan. Keep comparing the results day after day, week after week. Take pleasure in your "self-development" and thank God for it.

Is it that simple? Yes! Yet, like medicine, it helps only if it is taken regularly. It will probably be important, too, not to implement one self-improvement project after another. There will be some need for periods of inactivity, of "latency," to allow things to settle and to take root.

As the greatest help Ignatius recommends selecting a confidant or advocate. He encourages us to look for a person we trust and meet with that person to discuss our "self-improvement program" once every week over a period of four to six weeks. This will ensure success. Of course, it may also help greatly if we select someone who is also trying to dedicate their lives to the practice of creative self-development.

"TO LOOK FOR AND FIND GOD IN EVERYTHING"

Omnia ad majorem Dei gloriam (All to the greater glory of God) is the motto of the Jesuits. Yet more intimate are the words of Ignatius, "To look for and find God in everything." In a letter to fellow students, he writes that the students ought to "practice looking for God's, our Lord's, presence in all things, for instance while speaking, walking, seeing, tasting, listening, thinking, simply in every thing they do, for God's majesty is in all things because of his presence, his works and his Being."

Unfortunately, Ignatius failed to explain in greater detail how one is to do all these simultaneously. Perhaps he wished to merely suggest that we are always and foremost "in God"; we are a part of his creation in the sense of the words from Acts: "In him we live and move and have our being" (Acts 17:28). Or did he mean to suggest that attentiveness to life which makes everything more and more transparent, as illustrated perhaps by Alfred Delp, S.J.:

> *The world is full of God. He reaches for us from the pores of all things. Yet we remain frequently blind. We get bogged down in beautiful and in evil hours*

*and fail to probe them all the way to the source
from where they emanate from God. This is true of
all beautiful things and also of misery. God means
to celebrate our encounter with him in everything;
he is asking the questions and demands that we
respond with adoration and dedication. The trick,
and the task, is to make these insights and bless-
ings permanent in our consciousness and attitudes.
Then, and only then, will life be set free in the freedom we have frequently sought.*

The testimony of this freedom dates from those evil
hours in the Gestapo prison in Berlin, and that is why
it is all the more credible.

CONTEMPLATIVE ACTIVISM

Those in charge at Benedictine monasteries and
Ignatian retreat houses find a calmness under stress,
liveliness in everyday life, and faith in action. Catchy
spiritual mottos such as "struggle and contemplation"
(Taize), or the search for "engaged serenity" (Teilhard
de Chardin) echo that assumption that contemplation
and action go together.

Jerome P. Nadal, a member of the first generation
of Jesuits, described it as "contemplative action" and
"a higher active life." These, he stated, are characteris-
tic of Ignatian spirituality. What is meant by these concepts is the "discovery of the contemplative heart." It
beats whenever my activities are characterized by
trust, quiet, hope, inner freedom, etc. It is not unlike
the fundamental moods of being in love or of being
healthy. Ignatius talks about devotion—loving surrender in everything—as the highest level on which to
lead one's life.

Aids for developing a contemplative life:

- Get in touch with your own depth and with the "contemplative moments" of life.
- Avoid stuffing yourself with experiences; instead, leave some room and times for spiritual digestion.
- Develop the art of "enjoying" those numerous small breaks between telephone conversations, different tasks at work, walks down the stairs, and bus rides.
- Allow sufficient time for sleep and recreation.
- Cultivate downtime and simple, quiet moments.
- Take occasional advantage of short retreats—a day or a weekend.

Blessed Brother Franz Garrate, S.J., was once asked: "How can you be so calm in the midst of all of the hustle and bustle caused by requests, phone conversations, etc.?" He promptly replied: "I do what my strength allows me to do; whatever goes beyond that, I hand over to the Lord who can do everything. With his help, everything is easier, in fact pleasant. Don't we serve the best of all masters?"

117

POSTSCRIPTS: ON DEVELOPING A TASTE FOR RETREATS

In the event that you might have developed a taste for retreats while reading this book or while practicing some of its suggestions, some additional hints may help smooth the way. Just as the book started out with some prefatory remarks, it shall conclude with a postscript.

HOW CAN I PREPARE MYSELF FOR A RETREAT?

The desire for *Spiritual Exercises* which you may have experienced while reading or living this book's suggestions is certainly a sign that *Spiritual Exercises* might be quite helpful for you. Yet it may be wise for most people who are still highly unfamiliar with the practical side of venturing on a path of prayer, meditation, and other spiritual exercises to begin by participating in meditation weekends, brief retreats, retreats with an emphasis on community activities, etc. Only then consider going on a weeklong or even a thirty-day individual retreat. Some other suggestions include:

- It might be prudent to talk to people who have been on retreats. Your own retreat will be different, yet you can always learn from others if you keep an open mind.

- In addition to *Spiritual Exercises* and the autobiographical *A Pilgrim's Journey,* there are several good and easy-to-read introductions to Ignatian spirituality. Worth mentioning, for instance, are: *Finding God in All Things* by William Barry, S.J., from Ave Maria Press, *The Way of Ignatius Loyola,* edited by Philip Sheldrake, S.J., from the Institute of Jesuit Sources, *Inner Compass* by Margaret Silf, from Loyola Press, and *Thirty Days* by Paul Mariani from Penguin Books.

- Reading biographies of people who chose spiritual journeys of their own can be helpful. Those who rarely read the Bible might want to spend the days leading up to a retreat by reading it with greater intensity.
- Allow more time for personal prayer and meditation.
- Take stock of the time since your last retreat, or even of a longer period in your life.
- Raise your consciousness by evoking, through inner images and words, the meaning of desire and the hopes you associate with retreats.
- Ask yourself questions such as: What am I looking forward to? Is there anything that I am afraid of?
- If you have a spiritual companion, it may make sense to anticipate in a brief introductory discussion your expectations about the retreat. Furthermore, it may be beneficial to engage in a spiritual conversation with a good friend.
- If possible, it will be worth your while to cut back your activities during the days leading up to the retreat, so that you won't have to come to a screeching halt prior to its beginning.

ENGAGING IN A PRELIMINARY CONVERSATION

In most cases, it will be advisable to engage in a preliminary conversation prior to a retreat. If there is enough time to do so, it might be quite helpful because it will likely broaden the foundation of one's trust. This will be particularly important if one goes on an extended retreat, is still not sufficiently acquainted with the companion, or if this is the first time one ventures on a retreat. Normally, the following questions will arise:

- What do I think might be helpful during an initial conversation—for myself or for the companion? What am I willing to share freely?
- Who am I really? This involves general information about what I do, my family, and the denomination to which I belong.
- Have I been on retreats in the past? What was particularly helpful during these retreats? What caused problems for me?
- What characterizes me and my situation? My life and my faith?
- How much can I take on psychologically? Was I, or am I currently, in therapy? How is my health?
- How is my prayer life? Do I have different ways of praying? Where do I run into difficulties?
- What does the Bible, and reading the Bible, mean to me?
- Am I facing an important decision? Perhaps several decisions?
- Is there anything else I wish to add?
- Do I have any questions for the companion or about the retreat?

If a preliminary conversation will not be possible, a telephone conversation or a letter should suffice.

Trusting that God's Spirit will entice us and manifest itself in us throughout the *Spiritual Exercises* and in the exercises throughout one's entire life is probably even more important than being well prepared

TRAPS IN RETREATS

We may sometimes perceive our lives as continuously rising and falling. This happens also during retreats. Here are some typical traps:

- *To put pressure on oneself to see results.* Certainly, spiritual exercises are supposed to help us make decisions; however, it will be frequently counterproductive if we are convinced that at the end of a retreat decisive changes are to occur. Decisions are not like trees to be felled. They must be given time to mature. Then a gentle twist will be enough to make them happen. All in good time.
- *To imitate and repeat a pattern instead of following along a path of one's own.* There are certainly patterns, processes, and steps. Yet no retreat will be the same, just like no day is like any other. It will be important to experience surprises and to live in response to them. It will be equally counterproductive to constantly ask oneself about the phase one is currently in.
- *Immature surrender of responsibility.* As helpful as a reliable spiritual companion may be, therein also lurks the danger of delegating to him or her one's own responsibility for one's journey. By the grace of God and the Spirit—I am primarily responsible for my life. Others can be of help, but they cannot take my place.
- *Projection and transference.* With spiritual companionship, there is often a risk of projecting

problems, such as problems with authority, onto a new companion. Such projection and transference sometimes explains particularly strong reactions to new events or companions. Even a companion must be constantly vigilant as soon as he or she becomes aware of the presence of strong inner movements: which of these will be more helpful to understanding the other person? And what is overly idiosyncratic and likely to falsify the "objective" comprehension of an event in the other person?

• *Spiritual competition.* How far along am I when compared to the other exercitants? Do I have the best teacher? Am I about to adopt the best method or school? Am I still among the beginners, the advanced, or the perfect ones? It is human nature to ask all of these and additional questions, but they belong to the kind of nonsense the German mystic, Johannes Tauler (ca. 1300–1361), recommends to spread on the "field of God's will" before it stinks up one's stables; there it can serve as splendid fertilizer.

• *"Nobody can be as bad as I."* Anyone who has ever served as a companion during a retreat knows that statements such as these must be taken seriously. It is an expression of how a person feels. Yet, those who say that must be made to realize that one cannot even be the greatest of all sinners, because the more miserable a person, the greater the amount of God's love that will manifest itself in him or her.

• *To "go" on retreat instead of simply letting the retreat happen.* The active side of a retreat, i.e., the "going" on retreat and "doing a retreat" make good sense. Yet, it will be even more important to "let the retreat unfold." I like to announce at the beginning of a retreat: "The mystery of existence must be allowed to reveal itself." Thus we honor the name of God whose name is "I am who I am."

VARIATIO DELECTAT—"VARIETY BRINGS JOY"

Occasionally, a retreat may turn into a rut, lacking original freshness and challenge. Change may remedy this situation: To go on retreat at a different location or to change from a male to a female companion. Even the format of the retreat may be different. How about a "retreat with community elements;" a backpacking retreat, or "alone and on foot" (Ignatius); a week of studying the Bible in the mountains; a "retreat in the street," i.e. meditations in the midst of social hotspots in a city; a retreat at a homeless shelter, that is a retreat under the most primitive conditions.

At the same time, one could ask oneself if a course on how to communicate within the family would not be more helpful than mediations on the theme of "Love your Neighbor." Could not a series of conversations with a professional counselor over a period of an entire year help prepare for an important decision? What about a "conflict-resolution" seminar? Could I use some therapy? Or do I need to go on a decent vacation?

Maybe a retreat based entirely on silence (silent meditations), or prayers from the heart might help me gain profundity and simplicity.

PRACTICAL DETAILS

Nobody will be able to accuse this book of subliminally advertising retreats. The popularity of retreats is too obvious, and should a reader "catch fire," it is only fair to conclude with a few practical suggestions, to the practical questions that face every potential retreatant: Where? With whom? When?

Many parishes carry diocesan advertisements informing about a variety of retreats. Certainly, the parish priest will be familiar with programs offered by some religious or by spiritual communities.

Two good listings of Jesuit retreat resources can be found on the Internet. The first can be found at www.americamagazine.org/retreats.cfm. This Web site has some basic information on various retreat houses and is maintained by the Jesuit magazine *America*. An even better resource is at the Web site the Jesuits in the United States, www.jesuit.org. If you access the menu on the left of the screen, going to Resources and then to the sub-head of Spirituality, this will take you to an excellent page of Jesuit retreat resources.

Willi Lambert, S.J., is a retreat director and the spiritual consultant for the Community of Christian Life in Augsburg, Germany. Possessing a doctorate in theology, he is the author of many articles and books in German. This is his second book to be translated into English.

CPSIA information can be obtained
at www.ICGtesting.com
Printed in the USA
BVHW042133050220
571601BV00007B/116

9 781594 710346